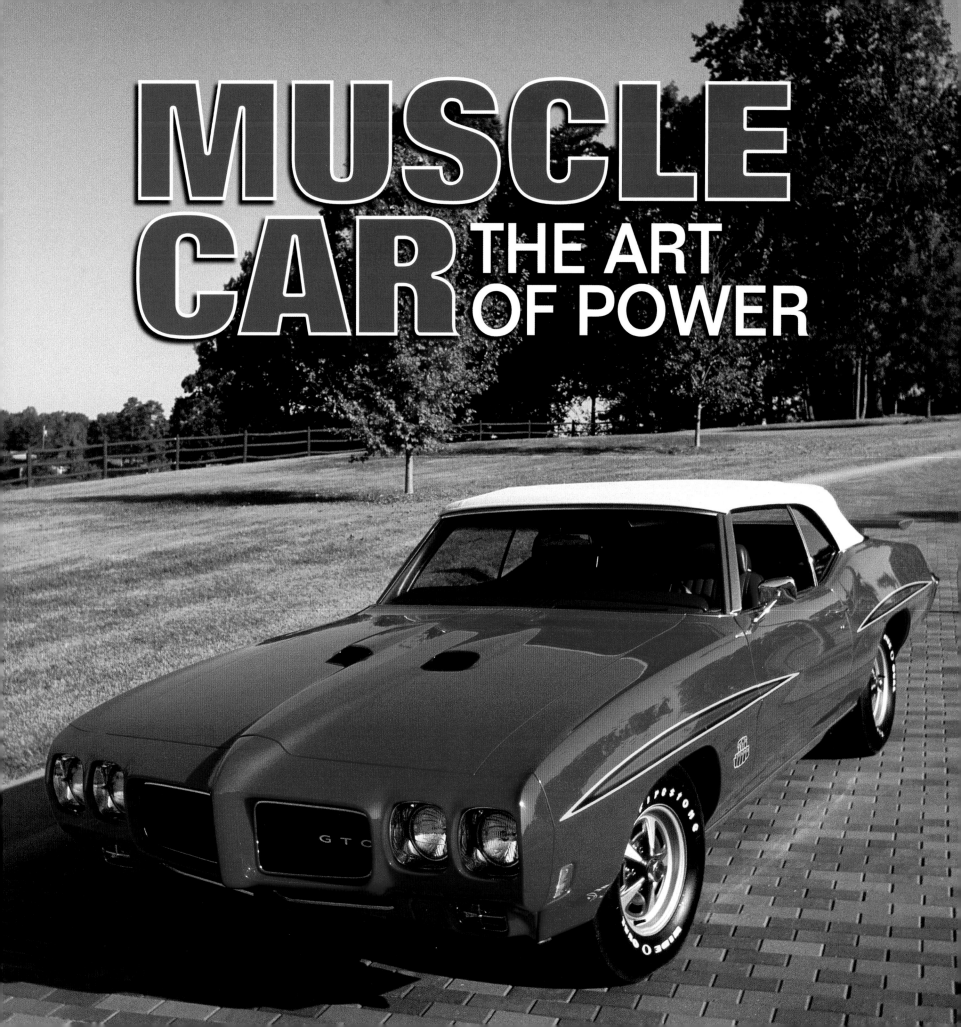

MUSCLE CAR
THE ART OF POWER

©2008 Krause Publications

Published by

krause publications
An Imprint of F+W Publications

700 East State Street • Iola, WI 54990-0001
715-445-2214 • 888-457-2873
www.krausebooks.com

Our toll-free number to place an order or obtain
a free catalog is (800) 258-0929.

Library of Congress Control Number: 2008928402

ISBN-13: 978-0-89689-617-8
ISBN-10: 0-89689-617-X

Designed by Kara Grundman
Edited by Paul Kennedy

Printed in China

Dedication:

To Lizzie, Katie and Cassie, with all my love. You girls are "awesome."

Other KP Automotive Titles

Contents

Introduction

When Detroit combined great looks with power our hearts — and cars — raced.

What is the fascination we have with muscle cars, their beauty and their power?

It all began in the early 1960s when automakers started producing special high-performance models of standard cars. These cars were an American response to the imported sports cars that were stealing sales away from Detroit. Austin-Healeys, MGs and Triumph TRs were built to provide fun driving, quick acceleration and the handling of a racecar. The thing is, they had small engines.

Sporty American cars adopted some sports car features like bucket seats, stick shifts, special suspension parts and stickier tires, but tossed in massive V-8 engines with extreme amounts of horsepower. These new models sent automotive writers scrambling for new terms to identify them and after toying with "supercar," the name "muscle car" was born. And what a beautiful birth it was.

Big, extra-powerful cars like the Olds 88, Chrysler 300, Plymouth Fury, Ford Thunderbird, Chevy Impala and Pontiac Bonneville pointed in the same direction as muscle cars, but didn't quite nail the formula. They put big-cube, big-horsepower engines in big cars. Then, in 1964, Pontiac's John Z. DeLorean got the brilliant idea of sneaking a big-block performance engine into one of the then-new mid-size cars. This concept gave us the first GTO and created the muscle car market.

DeLorean, with the help of Jim Wangers, broke the rules and came out ahead for it. The GTO sold much better than anyone expected it to and even the GM "bean counters" could see the muscle car was a success against all odds. Pretty soon, every automaker in America had a GTO clone in its model line-up. There was then a push to build muscle cars in every size class to try to expand the market, but the muscle car concept really only worked well on mid-size cars and "pony cars" in the style of the Mustang. There was simply no getting around the idea that a big engine in a small body was a thing of beauty.

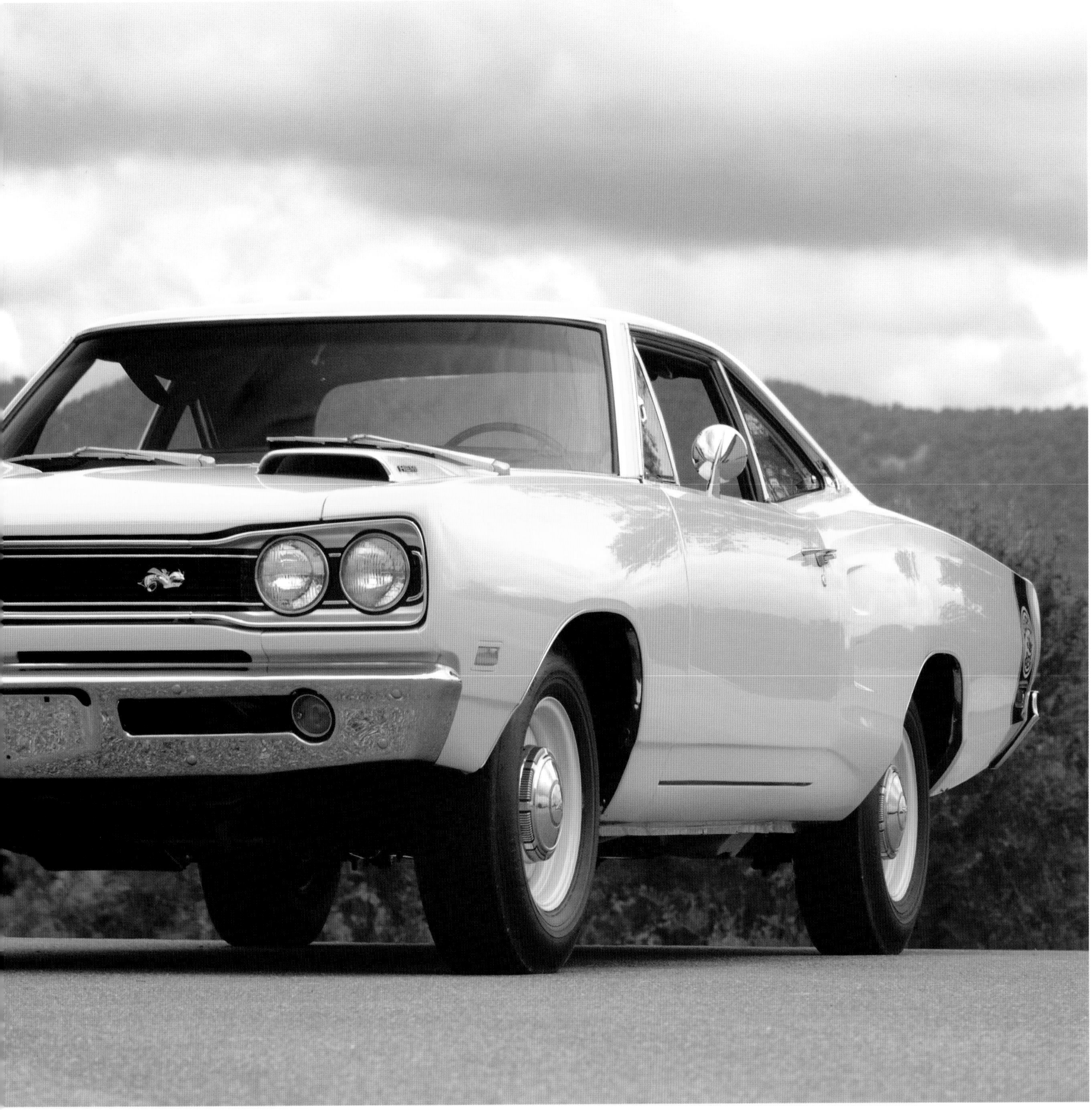

1969
Hurst
SS/AMX
Fastback Coupe

The SS/AMX option was sold on an "as is" basis, with no warranty.

The most interesting and sought-after AMX of all time was the '69 SS/AMX. Only 52 were sent from the AMC factory in Wisconsin to Hurst Performance Products in Pennsylvania. Purpose of the side trip: "legalization" for drag racing.

A pair of 650-cfm Holley four-barrels on an Edelbrock aluminum cross-ram intake topped the beefy SS/AMX 390. Doug's Headers and other modifications resulted in a conservative output of 340 hp.

The SS/AMX models went to NHRA and AHRA competitors, with Shirley Shahan — the "Drag-On-Lady" — perhaps the most famous. One of Shirley's brighter qualities was that she was pretty, pert and fetching when she stepped out of her racing cars. This remarkable young lady outraced many of her male competitors, but her cars always looked neat and clean. They were well maintained by her husband H.L. Shahan.

■ *Only 52 SS/AMX coupes were sold. The basic vehicle was manufactured at the AMC factory in Wisconsin then shipped to Hurst Performance Products in Pennsylvania to be turned into a drag machine.*

■ *The special 390-cid V-8 in the SS/AMX 390 carried two 650-cfm Holley four-barrel carburetors on an aluminum cross-ram intake sourced from Edelbrock. A pair of Doug's Headers helped the spent gases exit.*

In 1965, Shirley took an H.L.-prepared Super Stock Plymouth to a Winternationals Eliminator title. When the pair switched over to American Motors products in 1969, it wasn't long before Shirley established new D/Super Stock records with her SS/AMX. When the records were broken, the Drag-On Lady went back and set new marks for the same class in 1970.

Thanks to a recent offering on eBay, some added facts have come out about these cars. The seller offered photocopies of 20 pages of original American Motors Service Bulletins sent to Butch Jones, of Jones Rambler, in Nederland, Texas. The documents related SS/AMX No. 40, which has been owned by Edgars, Daimond, Dalley and other enthusiasts.

The bulletins reveal more about the cars than many books. They indicate that the cars were released on March 26, 1969. The retail price page shows $5,979 for either the Frost White P-72 SS/AMX or the same model in AMC racing colors of red, white and blue. It indicates that VINs began with 9M397X213560.

The SS/AMX option was sold on an "as is" basis, with no warranty. The cars came with the 390-engine, a functional cold-air hood scoop, an Edelbrock cross ram manifold and Lakewood traction bars.

Since racing helped sell cars in the '60s, the automakers often appointed product specialists to oversee racing activities. Ed Flannigan was AMC's Performance Specialist & Activities Director. The bulletins being sold on eBay contained a letter from Ed about the racing cars, as well as a scribbled notation on one memo showing Flannigan's "hot line" number.

The bulletins included NHRA racing rules, updates and memos. There were Western Union telegrams. The bulletins covered the front suspension, rear suspension, rear axle, tires, transmission, Crane camshaft (with a memo from Crane Cams), the clutch-and-flywheel assembly, electrical aspects of the 390-cid V-8, ram-air induction, head gaskets and the clutch housing.

PICTURE PERFECT DETAIL:

A "for-racing-only" car. Not street legal. Hot 390-cid AMC V-8 with forged steel crank to keep engine together under stress. Dual-quad carbs on special Edelbrock cross-ram intake. Meaty Schiefer clutch and P-plate. Hurst Competition Plus shifter for Borg-Warner T-10 four-speed manual transmission. Red, White and Blue paint. Sports-car-like, two-place seating and drag racing pedigree. One-year-only collectability and low production total.

■ *The SS/AMX cars were sold without a factory warranty. The SS/AMX package included the 390-cid V-8, a functional ram-induction hood scoop, a special cross-ram intake manifold and traction bars to give the tires bite.*

1969 Hurst SS/AMX

■ *The SS/AMX models were made for drag racing. Drag-On Lady Shirley Shahan was one of the most popular drivers of these hit cars. AMC stole her driving skills away from Chrysler.*

■ *Dick Bridges of Rockhill, South Carolina, owns this 1969 SS/AMX. Each car came with a dash plaque and a consecutive unit number. This beauty was the 50th car built in the series.*

There were illustrations, like one showing a special oil pan. Another depicted the carburetor/throttle linkage for the STR-11 cross-ram, dual four-barrel intake. There was also an illustration of the rear fender opening that shows where to alter the wheel wells. Welding repairs to the rear axle/spring perch were illustrated.

Problems such as piston wrist pin failure were discussed and there were even July 28, 1969, instructions on how to compute the compression ratio. Hurst issued a message about proper break-in procedures, which were special for these cars. On Sept. 18, 1969, Flannigan updated owners about the Super Stock clutch and pressure plate.

Numerous NHRA updates were issued. An Oct. 10, 1969, bulletin focused on intake valves. On April 3, 1970, Flannigan advised SS/AMX owners about a March 1, 1970, NHRA Technical Information Form that had to be filled out and returned. It included specific part numbers.

At least seven telegrams with further information updates were issued about SS/AMX cars. The topics covered included head gaskets, cylinder head volume, error messages, deck clearance and more.

■ *Because these hot AMX's were made for racing, AMC issued lots of technical bulletins that recommended modifications needed to go faster or meet new rules. Few of the cars remain as they left the factory.*

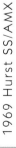

1969 Hurst SS/AMX

1974
AMC
Javelin 401
Two-Door Hardtop

Cute, sleek and with the hottest V-8 AMC
offered, this pony could gallop.

From 1971 on, the American Motors Javelin came in two different models: Javelin and AMX. Both cars were now four-passenger body styles. The preferred muscle car engine for the high-performance set was a new 401-cid V-8 that evolved from the sturdy old AMC 390-cid V-8.

First seen in 1968, the 390-cid V-8 was a 90-degree overhead valve engine like other AMC power plants. It had a cast iron cylinder head and engine block. With a 10.2:1 compression ratio and a single four-barrel carburetor, this motor generated 315 hp. This would later climb to as high as 340 hp in cars like the AMC Rebel "Machine."

AMC released its huge 401-cid V-8 in mid-size Matadors in 1971. Later, the automaker made it available in the Javelin-AMX. It debuted by the next season and, after that, it remained available through 1974. It was the most powerful V-8 that AMC ever used, although the 401-powered cars were not the fastest AMC models ever. This was because their weight was up a bit due to added anti-pollution and safety equipment.

■ *John Thompson of Denver, Colorado, is the proud owner of this two-door hardtop 1974 AMC Javelin.*

Trans-American Road Racing image. Cute, sleek styling with a racing-derived low-drag front end. Zippy paint, fancy seat and carpeting. Big-block V-8 power. The hottest V-8 American Motors Corporation ever offered, though not the fastest AMC car due to weight gains. Good-looking and sporty.

■ *The AMC 401–cid V-8 made the Javelin-AMX quick, despite its large 4-place size and heavier weight. The cars had to move about 13 pounds per horsepower, but were only a tad slower than 1968-1970 Javelin 390s.*

Naturally, the AMC 401-cid V-8 made the small Javelin-AMX a real muscle car, despite its larger four-place size and heavier weight. The AMX had started out as a two-passenger car, which was much lighter and could go pretty fast with a 390 V-8 under its hood.

The 401-engine had a 4.17 x 3.68-inch bore and stroke, a four-barrel carburetor and a 9.5:1 compression ratio. It developed 330 hp at 5200 rpm and 430 ft. lbs. of torque at 3300 rpm.

By 1973-1974, the power rating of the 401 was given as 255 net hp. With this engine, the Javelin-AMX tested for 0 to 60 mph in 7.7 seconds. It could do a quarter mile in 15.5 seconds at 90 mph. Its all-out top speed was 115.53 mph.

Both the Javelin and the Javelin-AMX could be equipped pretty much the same way, but the AMX had a distinctive looking flush style grille with a wire screen insert. In contrast, the Javelin's had a more conventional recessed style grille. The AMX also had a standard rear deck lid spoiler. Both cars featured a static bumper system with reinforced bumper guards and rear bumpers that were beefed up to withstand a new 5-miles per hour federal impact standard.

■ *Front bucket seats and a console were standard fare in both the Javelin and AMX. Javelin buyers also got manually operated front disc brakes as standard equipment.*

■ *After 1971, Javelins and AMXs shared bodies. The AMX had a cowl-induction hood, spoilers, badges and special trim. The muscle-car mill was the 401, which made the '74 Javelin-AMX a screamer.*

American Motors buyers could only get a four-speed manual gearbox with the 401-cid V-8 or the 360-cid four-barrel V-8. An automatic transmission was also an option. Only the AMX could be ordered with optional Rally Pack instrumentation, which *Road Test* Magazine described as "somewhat garish and not in keeping with the rest of the tastefully done interior."

Front bucket type seats and a center convenience console were standard fare in both the Javelin and the AMX. Javelin buyers also got standard manual disc brakes.

A problem *Road Test* discovered with these cars was an annoying wind roar when driving at highway speeds. The magazine's test driver, Jean Calvin, attributed this noise to the massive rain gutter that ran around the doors and the top of the windshield.

These cars came with a lot of options; everything from sporty "boat paddle" body side striping packages for $37.50, to a vinyl roof for $87.85. The Rally gauges were $77.45 extra. Some of the more expensive Javelin options were air conditioning for $377.45 extra and an AM/FM stereo radio for $195.60 extra.

Toward the end of the model year, in the fall of 1974, the Javelin was discontinued. When it left, the 401-powered version went, too. Sales of these cars — especially the big-block — had been absolutely dismal after the Arab Oil Embargo of 1973 kicked in. But AMC did stick to its guns until the bitter end and never discontinued the high-performance 401 muscle car engine until the pony car model was completely gone.

■ *After 1971, the 401 was de-tuned a bit for unleaded gas. It had 255 net hp. Javelins with the 401 were still pretty hot cars. Javelin-AMX output increased to 3,220 in 1972 and 5,707 in 1973, before tapering to 4,980 in 1974.*

1974 AMC Javelin 401

17

1965
Dodge
Coronet
Super Stock
Race Hemi

"Win on Sunday, Sell on Monday"
became the Dodge battle cry.

The 1965 model was not your "father's Coronet" of the mid- to late-1950s. Instead of having eyebrows and tailfins, it had last year's cantilevered hardtop roofline with a boxy body. It was based on the 1964 Polara, but had an inch longer stance.

The wheelbase was 117-in., unless you got your hands on a Super Stock version or an altered-wheelbase, factory-experimental A/FX drag car. Street cars had quad headlights. Coronet, Deluxe, 440 and 500 models were marketed. Although you could get the Hemi in any model, it was a pricey extra and most went into the cheaper coupes and two-door hardtops. Chrome trim and emblems didn't win races.

■ *Ed Strzelecki of Rochester, Michigan, is the owner of this black beauty. Introduced in 1965, the mid-sized Coronet became the centerpiece of Dodge Division's muscle car history. An advertisement that ran that year asked "Why not drop a Hemi in the new Coronet 500?"*

New model. Inexpensive, mid-size car. Lightweight for drag racing to the point of replacing four-headlight grille with two-headlight style to cut weight. The chassis and frame were lightened and beefed-up for racing. Rear axle shuffled forward. Improved 90-pounds-lighter Hemi engine. Requires racing gas or aviation fuel to run properly. Plain-Jane "street" car looks with racing-only engineering.

■ *The 1965 Dodge Coronet was in the last year of a styling cycle. It continued to use a 117-inch wheelbase chassis and had an overall length of 204 inches.*

Dodge offered a wide variety of engines in Coronets, from a six-cylinder to a list of V-8s as long as your arm. You could get them with 273, 318, 361, 383 or 426 cubic inches. Early in the model year, the 426 was a "wedge," but in December 1964, Dodge put an advertisement in *Hot Rod* magazine that promoted a new engine of similar displacement. "Our new 426 Coronet ought to have its head examined," the copywriters teased. At the same time, they asked, "Why not drop a Hemi in the new Coronet 500?"

Chrysler New Yorkers, Imperials and 300 Letter Cars of the 1950s had offered a Hemi V-8, a very powerful engine. Lots of dragsters of the era were fitted with Chrysler "Firepower" Hemis or with comparable Dodge or De Soto Hemi engines of different displacement. Those cars did well on the street, as well as on NASCAR tracks and drag strips. But the mid-1965 Hemi was different. It had a 12.5:1 compression ratio, which essentially meant it was for racing use only. Street gas wouldn't do in those environs.

426-Wedge-powered Dodges with special lightweight aluminum body panels had torn up many drag strips during 1964. When the National Hot Rod Association's rules changed, a minimum weight of 3,400 pounds was required. Aluminum was out. So Dodge built an all-steel car that could win under the new regulations. This Super Stock Coronet was a two-door sedan with the rear axle moved forward two inches, putting more weight on the rear wheels.

■ *The Super Stock Dodge Coronets became pretty famous drag racing cars in 1965. The Ramchargers, a dedicated team of talented drivers who won many races and series championships, piloted the Dodges.*

■ *Dodge placed an ad in **Hot Rod** that promoted a new engine having the same displacement as the 426 Wedge, but it was a Hemi. The advertisement read: "Our new 426 Coronet ought to have its head examined." Extra gauges helped monitor Hemi.*

A grille with two fewer headlight assemblies was another Super Stock weight-saving measure. Dodge also revamped the front cross member to lop off another 25 pounds. Aluminum and magnesium engine components were used to lighten the Hemi engine. The motor was around 90 pounds lighter. Behind it, Coronet racers could get a new column-shifted TorqueFlite automatic transmission or a four-speed manual gearbox with a floor shift.

The Super Stock Coronets became pretty famous drag racing cars in 1965, thanks to the Ramchargers, a dedicated team of talented drivers who won many races and series championships. The honors included Top Stock Eliminator and Mr. Stock Eliminator honors at the American Hot Rod Association Winter Championships in Phoenix, Arizona, and the S/SA class title at the National Hot Rod Association's Nationals.

In NASCAR, the Coronets did not fare as well as in drag racing. Bill France, Sr. banned them early in the season, which allowed big-block Fords to sweep up at many races. France later changed his mind a bit, and allowed Hemis to be used on mile-or-longer tracks only in cars with at least a 119-inch wheelbase. On shorter tracks only, they could be used in Coronets. In other words, the Hemi Coronets didn't put in any super speedway duty.

Coronets with the race Hemi were rare even when new. Today, they are hard-to-find collector cars that fetch high-dollar auction prices in the $90,000 to $150,000 range. Makes you cringe to think you could have bought one for less than $3,000 back in 1965!

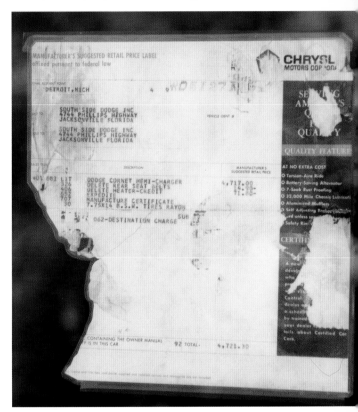

■ *"Win on Sunday, Sell on Monday" was the theme at Dodge Division in the early- to mid-1960s. Fans took note when these hot Dodges won races, especially when they could buy one similar to the drag race winners.*

1965 Dodge Coronet

1967
Dodge Hemi Charger

The Charger was aimed at buyer who wanted something sporty, but didn't want to give up room and comfort.

Beginning in 1966, the Charger was Dodge's entre to fastback fanatisim. The new model used the same mid-sized chassis and running gear components as the Coronet, but the Charger's body was completely different. The big fastback roof gave it the appearance of being a larger car.

The first Charger's frontal area was filled with a convex "electric shaver" grille with a large, round Charger crest in the center. A full-width taillight crossed the entire rear end of the car. It had the Charger name spelled out in in block letters that were evenly spaced across the lens. Hidden headlights were the rage and the Charger featured them. Two fine feature lines were used along the bodyside and the fastback ended at the rear of the car.

■ *The aerodynamic 1967 Dodge Charger was aimed at the sporty-car buyer who didn't want to give up room and comfort. Car owner Lonnie Shelton enjoys the size and speed of his Charger while tooling around his home in Pampa, Texas.*

■ *"Even Custer couldn't muster a stampede like this," is a slogan Dodge Division used to advertise the Hemi Charger. The word HEMI was proudly displayed on the car's flanks in small block letters.*

■ *The 1967 Dodge Chargers were much rarer than the original 1966 models. Only 15,788 were built. This included 118 cars with the Hemi V-8 engine, of which half were had a four-speed manual gearbox.*

■ *Chargers offered many extras. With a four-speed transmission, a Sure-Grip axle was mandatory. A good idea for Hemi Chargers was 11-inch front disc brakes. They slowed the car down from 60 mph in just 133 feet.*

Bucket seats were standard front and rear. They were nestled on either side of a spaceship like, full-length center console. The seats in the back of the car folded individually to provide a spacious luggage compartment.

The instrument panel was unique to the Charger. It had four large, round pods containing all the instruments. They were located directly in front of the driver. A floor mounted shifter was used with both stick shift or automatic transmission cars. The shifter was located in the console that divided seats.

The Charger was aimed at buyer who wanted something sporty, but didn't want to give up room and comfort. Dodge assumed that the person interested in this car would be willing to spring for a bit extra to get bigger and more powerful engines. The base engine was a 318-cid 230-hp job that pushed the Charger from 0 to 60 mph in 10.9 seconds and down the quarter mile in 18.6 seconds at 76 mph.

With its slant toward competition in NASCAR and USAC, Dodge wanted the Charger to reflect its racing image and also offered it with a nice selection of optional, higher-performance V-8s. The second step up the ladder was a 383-cid 326-hp big-block V-8 that took the Charger from 0 to 60 mph in 8.9 seconds and down the quarter mile in 16.5 seconds at 86.4 mph. There was also the 440-cid 375-hp engine good for 0 to 60 mph in eight seconds and a 15.5-second quarter mile at 93 mph.

The top dog was the 426-cid 425-hp Hemi, which breathed through a pair of four-barrel carburetors. With this engine the Charger went 0 to 60 mph in 7.6 seconds and did the quarter mile in 14.4 seconds at 100 mph! The Hemi engine — option No. 73 — was an $877.55 extra in the Charger. When the Hemi was ordered, big brakes and the heavy-duty suspension were a requirement. The Hemi was not offered in conjunction with a three-speed manual gearbox.

You could get the Hemi with either a special type of TorqueFite automatic transmission or a four-speed manual. The Hemi three-speed TorqueFlite included a high-upshift speed governor. When a buyer ordered the four-speed manual transmission, a Sure Grip no-slip rear axle was mandatory. A good idea for the Hemi Charger was the addition of 11-inch front disc brakes, which could slow the hot Mopar down, from 60 mph, in an amazing 133 feet.

Only 15,788 1967 Chargers were built. This total included just 118 cars with the 426-cid Hemi V-8. Half of the Hemi cars were manufactured with a four-speed manual gearbox.

If you're considering buying a 1967 Hemi Charger today, you might appreciate knowing that it got 11.7 mpg in city driving and about 14.4 mpg on the open highway. Of course if you can afford one of these beauties, gas mileage — no matter the high prices at the pump — probably isn't a concern.

PICTURE PERFECT DETAIL:

Considered a "specialty model" by Dodge. The Hemi Charger was basically the mid-size Coronet with a radical fastback, but a lot more rare. One of the most exciting interiors of the muscle-car era reminded you of an amusement park "spaceship" ride. Great aerodynamics for the track. Standard features include a 150-mph speedometer, a 6,000-rpm tachometer and Blue Streak racing tires. Big brakes and heavy-duty suspension came with the Hemi engine package.

■ *The Hemi V-8 was an $877.55 option in the Charger. When ordered for a Hemi Charger, the three-speed TorqueFlite automatic transmission came with a special high-upshift speed governor.*

1967 Dodge Hemi Charger

1968
Dodge Dart GSS

To strengthen the cars to match the engine, the front frame cross member was upgraded.

GSS stood for "Grand Spaulding Special." Grand Spaulding Dodge, a performance-oriented new-car dealership, was located at 3300 W. Grand Ave. in Chicago, Illinois. Norman Kraus ran the place. He started selling cars in the early 1950s. In 1957, he placed a two-line classified ad in a newspaper to sell a stick-shift '56 Chevy ragtop. The shortness of the ad prompted him to put his name down as Mr. Norm and the moniker stuck.

Kraus gained local notoriety for selling hopped-up used cars. This prompted a Dodge rep to offer him a factory franchise in 1960, but he considered the cars "stodgy Dodgies" and turned the deal down. By late-1962, Dodge cars were getting more interesting and an advance peak at the '63 models inspired Kraus to "sign on the dotted line."

After some teething pains, Kraus got a suitable showroom to sell from and signed up to back a local racing car to promote sales. When the car won drag races, new customers flocked to Grand Spaulding Dodge wanting other cars like it.

■ *Many, if not all, GSS Darts had "383" badges on the front fender, although it was actually a 440 that got stuffed under the hood. Hurst, not Dodge, put the big engines into the cars.*

■ *The '68 Dart, like this one owned by Richard Myers, Wallaceburg, Ontario, used the same body introduced in 1967 with minor trim updates. The Dart name, in block letters, appeared along the sides of the rear fenders and " Dodge" was on the hood.*

■ *GSS stood for "Grand Spaulding Special." Grand Spaulding Dodge was a performance-oriented Dodge dealership on West Grand Ave. in Chicago. The GSS served as a prototype for the factory-built GTS.*

Kraus did so well moving performance cars that he started Mr. Norm's Sport Club. The dealership's super-tuned Dodges were a hit and Norm started building his own editions of factory models with added youth-market appeal. The 1968 Dodge Dart GSS was one of the more memorable products he concocted.

Conceptually, the car started when Norm got a sales call from the Dodge representative just before the 1967 models were due out. Mr. Norm thought that the new Dart looked great, but he wondered why it was only offered with smaller 273-cid V-8 and not the 383-cid big-block engine. "Gimme a break," he told the factory rep. "These things ain't going to eat a 396 Camaro's lunch."

Norm decided to make a Dart that could devour a Camaro. His formula was easy: buy a bunch of Darts, have a 440 Mopar engine fitted to them, beef-up the rest of the car and wait for the orders to roll in.

These cars were actually shipped, without drive trains, from the Dodge factory to Hurst Performance Products in Pennsylvania. Hurst installed a 440-cid four-barrel Chrysler V-8 and automatic transmission. Bumblebee striping usually decorated the

rear end of car. They had fat red stripe tires, special racing wheels, GSS badging and "Mr. Norm's" decals. In at least some cases, the engine call outs on the fender did not match the actual cubes under the hood.

To strengthen the cars to match the engine, the front frame cross member was upgraded. Heavy-duty suspension components were tossed into the mix and the left-hand side engine mounting was beefed up. The 440 engines also had special exhaust manifolds. Dual exhaust systems were a must, of course. Ditto strong wheels and fat tires.

Hurst records show that a total of only 48 Darts were converted to Dart GSS models and all of these cars were sent to Grand Spaulding Dodge to be sold. Several of the cars were put into the hands of car magazine editors for testing. Dodge engineers also utilized a Mr. Norm's GSS as their prototype for the factory's M-code 383-powered Dart GTS.

Kraus realized that these cars appealed mainly to drag racers, many of whom were located far from his Chicago dealership. So he checked with Continental Airlines and found he that it would cost $57 to fly from California to Chicago, on stand-by basis, at night. So he offered to pay that much airfare to anyone wishing to come to his dealership to pick up a GSS Dart. Whether anyone actually came isn't known, but the "free airfare" promotion certainly caused a stir at a time when most people had never flown on an airplane.

PICTURE PERFECT DETAIL:

Compact-sized Dodge. Powerful, torque-twisting 440-cid Mopar big-block V-8 stuffed into Dart engine bay. Heavy-duty everything. Modified front K-member. Featured special left-hand engine mounting, special exhaust headers and beefed-up TorqueFlite automatic transmission (no four-speed manual available in GSS Darts). Heavy-duty transmission clutch pack and racing-type valve body. Low (numerically higher) rear axle gear ratio. Prototype for Dodge's "factory hot rod" GTS Dart.

■ *The GSS was essentially a GTS and included GTS features like Firm-Ride shocks, heavy-duty Rallye suspension and E70-14 Red Streak tires. Bucket seats were standard in the hardtop.*

1968 Dodge Dart GSS

1969
Dodge Charger 500 Hemi

Charger 500s with automatics covered the quarter-mile in 14.01 seconds at 100 mph.

The 1969 Hemi Charger 500 was a NASCAR homologation special. Wind tunnel testing showed that the gorgeous, new-for-'68 Gen II Charger body had its drawbacks on high-speed NASCAR tracks. The showroom car created lots of wind turbulence when raced on super speedways. Not wanting to do a total redesign for racing, engineers did a prototype and found that the '68 Coronet grille was an easy swap. It fit flusher and reduced wind buffeting. A flush-mounted rear window was also used.

■ *The 1969 Charger continued to use the beautiful body that had debuted in 1968, but with a new taillight treatment. Charger 500 models were built to fulfill a NASCAR requirement for racing.*

■ *Dodge Charger 500s were based on the standard Charger, but had a unique radiator grille that was not recessed into the oval grille opening. Also specific to this model was a flush-mounted rear window glass.*

The "production" Charger 500 was not really a mass-produced car. It was a special model — based on the prototype — that was offered to make the racing modifications "legal" to NASCAR. If Dodge said is was going to make 500 cars with the same features for public sale, NASCAR would OK them. In reality, only 392 cars were made.

Chrysler said, "The Charger 500 is offered specifically for the high-performance race tracks. It is available only to qualified performance participants and is being built to order on a limited-production basis."

The handcrafted body modifications were done by Creative Industries, an aftermarket firm from Detroit, Mich. Though some books say Hemis were standard, 392 of these cars have been researched and only about nine percent had Hemis.

■ A minimum of 500 cars had to be sold to make the Dodge Charger 500 legal for racing under NASCAR rules. The model designation was based on the number of cars that Dodge was supposed to manufacture.

■ Charger 500s with automatic transmission did the quarter-mile in 14.01 seconds at 100 mph. Cars with four-speed manual transmission were significantly faster and did the quarter mile in 13.60 seconds at 107.44 mph.

1969 Dodge Charger 500 Hemi

33

■ *The handcrafted body modifications made to the Dodge Charger 500s were actually carried out by Creative Industries, an aftermarket-customizing firm located in Detroit, Michigan.*

Standard equipment did include a heavy-duty suspension, a four-speed manual gearbox (or TorqueFlite automatic), a rear bumblebee stripe, "500" model badges, a special shorter-than-stock deck lid and a custom-made package shelf.

Officially, 32 Hemi-powered cars were built, though experts have tracked down serial numbers for 35. Around 15 those had four-speed manual gearboxes. Charger 500s with automatics covered the quarter-mile in 14.01 seconds at 100 mph. Cars with optional four-speed transmissions were significantly faster. They did the quarter mile in 13.60 seconds at 107.44 mph.

John Lammers of Wainfleet, Ontario, Canada, spotted this Black Charger on his way home from work back in 1989. The car showed a mere 1,270 miles on its odometer. It had a serial number starting with "XX," which was Chrysler's code for its altered cars that were made for the NASCAR circuit.

John was told Reggie Jackson – a serious muscle car fan – had a deal pending to buy the car. So, he went back to see it a second time . . . and a third time. In fact, he went to see it every Monday thereafter.

Two months went by, and as luck would have it, the deal to sell the car to Reggie Jackson fell apart. Lammers had his Charger 500. In 10 years of ownership, Lammers has driven the car only 350 miles. Other than new tires, a new battery cable and a mouse-eaten headliner, the car is "factory" right down to its Super Performance Axle Package and 4.10 Dana rear end. It is probably the lowest-mileage Charger 500 left on the planet. Inside, the red upholstery, dash and carpet are in near mint condition. The paint is original and looks beautiful. It's a rolling time capsule of originality.

PICTURE PERFECT DETAIL:

Flush-mounted '68 Coronet grille. Rear window glass moved up to match angle of rear roof pillars, with fiberglass "plug" fitted below and blended in. Trunk lid shortened accordingly with hinges re-positioned. Rear window package shelf modified. Car featured bumblebee racing stripe with "500" graphics. Books say the 426 Hemi was the only engine, but historians say otherwise. Mid-year, limited production model.

■ *Literature said the Charger 500 was offered specifically for high-performance racing tracks and available only to qualified race drivers. This brought buyers flocking to Dodge dealerships to buy one of the hot cars.*

1969 Dodge Charger 500 Hemi

1969
Dodge
Coronet
Super Bee

The Coronet series started with your basic Deluxe Coronet.

"Right out of the box, the Super Bee lives up to its decals," said *Car Life*. "And it's a honey of a low-budget Supercar." The editors seemed to like everything about the car, except its clock-shrouded tach and flat front seat.

The Coronet series started with your basic Deluxe Coronet. Next up the ladder was the Coronet 440 with carpeting and wheel lip moldings. The Coronet 500 added a V-8 and fancy features (and bucket seats in hardtops). The Super Bee was like a slightly stripped-down Coronet 500 that got "hot rodded" under the hood. Since Chrysler had a lot invested in the four-speed gearbox, TorqueFlite automatic transmission was only $39.30 extra.

Car and Driver used a four-barrel 383 Super Bee in a comparison of six "econo-racers." It had a 3.55:1 limited-slip differential ($102.15), power disc brakes ($93.10), head restraints ($26.50), foam-padded seats ($8.60), TorqueFlite ($40.40), a remote-adjustable mirror ($9.65), three-speed windshield wipers ($5.40),

■ *Our feature car is a rare Hemi-powered Dodge Super Bee. The dual-four-barrel "Street Hemi" V-8, option code E74, was a racing engine that was slightly de-tuned for street use.*

■ *Dealer cost for the Hemi engine was $673.55 and the retail price for the option was $830.65. The A36 Performance Axle package was $64.40 on Super Bees, but came standard with the Hemi V-8.*

■ ***Car Life*** *magazine (February 1969) described the Coronet Super Bee as a "first-cabin" road car. It was a well-balanced muscle car with a firm, safe ride that could surprise a sports car on a mountain road.*

undercoating ($16.60), rear quarter air scoops ($35.80), rear bumper guards ($16), a tachometer and clock ($50.15), cold air induction ($73.30), AM radio ($63.35), power steering ($97.65), styled wheels ($88.55) and F70 x 14 tires. The car did 0-to-60 mph in 5.6 seconds and the quarter mile in 14.04 seconds at 99.55 mph. The magazine found Chrysler had "tweaked" the car with dual-point distributor and fat-pipe exhausts. "We can't consider our test car's performance to be representative of a 383 Super Bee you would buy," it admitted.

There were two Super Bees. The new WM23 two-door hardtop had a $3,138 starting price. The WM21 coupe returned with a $3,076 window sticker. *Car Life* described the Super Bee's standard 335-hp 383 four-barrel V-8 as a balanced power plant with power to "put the back of the car in line with the front on turns, but not enough to convert forward motion into sideways motion during vigorous driving." The test car, a hardtop, did 0 to 60 in 6.6 seconds and the quarter mile in 14.73 seconds at 95.5 mph.

During the model year, the "Six-Pack" option with three two-barrel Holley carbs on an aluminum Edelbrock manifold was introduced. Cars so equipped generated 390 hp and 490 foot-pounds of torque. The Six-Pack option included a flat black fiberglass hood that locked in place with four chrome pins. This allowed the hood to be removed quickly, which weekend drag racers loved.

The legendary Hemi had a 4.25 x 3.75 bore and stroke for 426 cubic inches. With a 10.25:1 compression ratio and twin four-barrel carbs, it generated 425 hp at 5000 rpm. Hemi Super Bees also got a viscous-drive fan, a bigger radiator and a radiator fan shroud. *Car Life* tested a Hemi Charger 500 (very similar to a Super Bee) and managed a 5.7-second 0 to 60 run and a 13.68-second quarter-mile pass at 104.8 mph.

Also new for 1969 was the Ramcharger Air Scoop Hood, a $73.30 option that was standard equipment on Hemi Super Bees. It had two large hood-mounted air scoops, an under hood air plenum and a switch to select between warm and cold air. To get this option you had to also get three-speed wipers.

Car Life gave gold stars to its test car's engine performance and said that the TorqueFlite automatic did everything well with quick, positive shifts. It found the brakes well suited to stopping such a muscle machine. Also rated positive was the car's size and trunk space. In summary, the Super Bee proved to be a good road car, as well as a top-notch grand touring car.

A total of 27,800 Coronet Super Bees were built in the 1969 model year. Of these, 166 were Hemi-powered cars and 92 of the Hemis came with the four-speed manual transmission.

PICTURE PERFECT DETAIL:

Same as Charger 500, except no Light Group, pedal dress-up trim, panel appliqué and extra-thick seat cushions. Standard engine is 383-cid big-block V-8 with 440-type heads (Hemi V-8 optional), heavy-duty 11-inch drum-type brakes, Rallye suspension system with sway bar, Firm-Ride shock absorbers, power-bulge hood, bumblebee stripes, F70-14 Red Line tires and standard four-speed manual transmission (TorqueFlite optional). A 70-amp heavy-duty battery was standard, as were manually adjusted heavy-duty brakes.

■ *The interior of the Super Bee had a nice simple array of mostly-easy-to-read dials right in front of the driver. However, the clock and tach were combined. The tach was in the center of the clock and thus hard to read.*

1969 Dodge Coronet

39

MUSCLE CAR • THE ART OF POWER

1970
Dodge Challenger R/T

Race car looks a hit
with muscle car buyers.

The aptly named Challenger put Dodge into the pony car business. Like the Mercury Cougar and the Pontiac Firebird, the Challenger was a kind of upscale version of a cheaper corporate cousin. It was a modified Plymouth Barracuda with a two-inch longer wheelbase, three inches more length and fancier trimmings. Its extra size made the Challenger a tad roomier.

Six Challenger models were marketed. In each case the model code started with a J. The second letter was an "H" for high line or an "S" for the higher-performance sports line. Then came the body style codes: 23 for two-door hardtop, 27 for convertible coupe or 29 for Special Edition hardtop. Available for both Challengers and Challenger R/Ts, the Special Edition group included a formal-style roof with a vinyl covering, an overhead interior consolette with warning lights and bucket seats with vinyl-and-leather trim.

■ *The '70 Challenger had smooth styling lines, but felt "too bulky" to period road testers. Hard, fast cornering activity could induce body lean, but the driver rarely felt it. The suspension felt refreshingly firm.*

PICTURE PERFECT DETAIL:

383 four-barrel V-8 (383 Magnum, 440 Magnum, 440 "Six-Pack" or Hemi optional), three-speed manual transmission with floor shift (base engine only), all-vinyl bucket seats with integral head restraints, 3-spoke simulated walnut steering wheel, concealed 2-speed electric wiper, wheel lip moldings, carpeting, heater and defroster, cigar lighter, glove box lock, instrument panel Rallye cluster, front and rear Rallye Pack suspension with sway bar, heavy-duty drum type brakes, F70-14 fiberglass blackwall tires with raised white letters and longitudinal tape stripe or bumblebee stripe.

■ *The R/T package included the elements that were essential to give the "racy car" look that muscle car buyers wanted. They included big air-intake scoops, bucket seats and a floor-mounted gear shifter,*

Basically, Dodge arranged the Challenger offerings so a buyer could get any engine with any body or interior. The anatomical features of the Challenger R/T, as listed above, made it the muscle car model with the bigger motors as standard fare. However, if you teamed the R/T with the SE, you then had a fancy muscle car with a vinyl roof and part-leather upholstery.

Challenger R/T buyers also had a choice of five engines, starting with the 330-hp four-barrel 383. The others were the 335-hp Magnum 383, the 375-hp Magnum 440, the 390-hp 440 Six-Pack and the 426 Hemi with two four-barrel carbs and 425 hp. The R/T with the 440 Six-Pack seemed to be the combination that got the heaviest push from Dodge, at least when it came to supplying magazine test cars. *Car Life* (December 1969) was provided with a purple R/T Six-Pack convertible, while *Road Test* got a R/T Special Edition hardtop with the same engine.

Car Life described the Challenger as a "condensed Charger" and noted that trying to stuff the larger car's components into a smaller package compromised "people room." The car's lowness and hard-to-see-out-of rear window did not go overlooked. The front seats were badly positioned and lacked lateral support; the rear seats were described as "impossible." Also criticized was the small trunk space. *Car Life's* car had mechanical problems, so its performance figures were off the mark. It still did 0 to 60

in 7.7 seconds and the quarter mile in as little as 14.64 seconds at 97.82 mph. On the plus side, the dash layout was praised. The tester also admitted, "The Challenger has a superior chassis, good brakes, we think successful styling and the best selection of engines in town."

In *Road Test's* report, the hardtop did the quarter mile in 15.72 seconds at 91.18 mph. It was noted these results were disappointing, possibly because the car was not broken in. The Special Edition roof reduced rear window glass and this didn't go unnoticed. "We found the new Challenger extremely comfortable to drive, and to handle exceptionally well by all but the most nit-picking yeah-but-have-you-ever-driven-a-Porsche standards," said the road tester, who also described the 440 Six-Pack as being "like an unleashed dragster."

Road Test found the leather Special Edition seats very comfortable, but had trouble with too much heat leaking into the cabin. This publication also found trunk space a bit tight.

The R/T hardtop listed for $3,266 and 14,889 were built. The convertible was $3,535 and 3,979 were made. Only 1,070 Challenger SEs, base-priced at $3,498, left the factory. Hemi production included 287 hardtops (137 with four-speeds), 60 SE hardtops (23 with four-speeds) and nine convertibles (five with four-speeds). All Hemi Challengers were R/Ts. Hemis did the quarter-mile in 14 seconds at 104 mph.

■ *The Rallye Instrument Panel supplied in Challenger R/T models had a full array of gauges to tell the driver all he needed to know. Front seat shoulder room was 56.2 inches.*

1964
Plymouth
426-R/426-S

This package was officially intended
for "off-road" use only.

Why change a good thing? In 1964 Chrysler's now historical Plymouth Division returned with the hairy "Super Stock" Max Wedge 426-cid V-8, but in a new "Stage III" state of tune. "Stage III" meant that it was the third edition of this potent power plant with another round of high-performance tweaks.

The year's improvements included larger-capacity Carter carburetors (two big four-barrels on a cast-aluminum ram-induction manifold were used), matching larger air cleaners, a new camshaft with 320 degrees of overlap, modified combustion chambers (with deeper clearance notches around the valves), 13.0:1 pistons replaced by 12.5:1 pistons in the higher-compression engine and new exhaust manifolds designed for NASCAR racing. The carbs had tuned, equal-length 21-in. passages that dumped into a pair of giant-size steel tubes that spat the gases into a fat head pipe on either side. This was what Chrysler called a "Tri-Y" setup and isn't something you're likely to see at your local swap meet.

This package was officially intended for "off-road" use only. That meant you were supposed to stick to putting your car on a trailer and pulling it to the drag strip on Sunday – not sneaking it out to the street races on Friday night. This $500 package had an "R" suffix

■ *Cars like this one were made for racing and should have a history behind them. Tracing and documenting this history can greatly increase a car's value as a collectible automobile.*

Plymouth racing cars used the stock body, but the drive train, brakes, chassis, suspension and wheel and tire equipment were beefed up to deal with the torque-twisting power of the 426 Max Wedge Stage III V-8.

PICTURE PERFECT DETAIL:

Restyled Plymouth body on 116-in. wheelbase. "Ramcharger" Stage III Super Stock 426-cid "wedge-head" V-8 with 425 hp thanks to lots of racing-type goodies. Featured a new, Chrysler-engineered full-synchro four-speed manual transmission with floor shifter. Big hood scoop. Heavy-duty underpinnings to handle the horsepower. Fat tires and stronger wheels. Often seen as a fast-moving blur with numbers on its side.

on its option code to show it was for racing. At 500 bucks it sounds cheap now, but that was a ton of money in 1964.

The Super Stock 426 came in the same two flavors it had before: 415 hp and 425 hp. New for the year, however, was a street-friendly 426-S edition of the 426 Wedge that advertised 365 horsepower. In all honestly, it actually produced about 410 "real world" horsepower, but who believes ads anyway?

This engine did not come with all of the "Max Wedge" racing hardware, but because of the similar cubic inch displacement numbers, many buyers thought it was nearly the same engine as the 426-R. It featured just a single four-barrel carburetor on a cast iron intake manifold and used only a 10.3:1 compression ratio. The dual exhaust system was of standard "high performance" design with twin, fat pipes. It was not a 426-R, but it was not to be sneezed at, either.

With 470 foot-pounds of torque at 3200 rpm, the 426-S engine was no slouch on the street or the drag strip. It was far happier on street gas and in everyday use than the "race" versions of the 426. Those tended to need lots of coddling and tuning, plus racing fuel or av gas that you can't get at a fillin' station. A lot of these engines went into higher-priced Plymouths that were loaded up with trim and options. The big spenders wanted the big engines, of course.

Most of 426-R engines, on the other hand, were bolted into entry-level Savoy two-door sedans because they were the cheapest and lightest Plymouths made. Why pay for chrome when you were saving to buy the expensive racing engine and chrome adds weight anyway, doesn't it? On the drag strip, a few less ounces of anything could add up to a win and a trophy.

There were also stock car racing versions of the 426-R supplied for NASCAR competition. Due to the sanctioning body's rules, these carried single four-barrel carburetors. The drag racers were permitted to run the dual-quad setup, which was best for short-mileage acceleration contests. They were plain-Jane machines, but amazingly fast with performance in the same range as 1963.

The street version of the 426 could be had in any model from the Savoy to the Sport Fury hardtop or convertible. A 1964 Sport Fury two-door hardtop with the 426-cid 365-hp V-8 carried about 9.5 pounds per horsepower and could turn in 6.8 seconds 0-to-60 mph runs. The same combination was good for a 15.2-second quarter mile run.

■ *These cars were as plain on the inside as they were on the outside. Many had the interior gutted to save weight. It was still necessary to have a tachometer and a full set of gauges to monitor the engine.*

1968
Plymouth Belvedere GTX
Hemi Convertible

A high horsepower, high
content muscle car beauty.

In February 1968, *Car Life* suggested that you could buy the most powerful, fastest stock automobile in America by simply visiting your Plymouth dealer and getting a GTX. The magazine liked both engines that the car came with and tested them both. The Hemi was faster, but it required higher engine speeds to deliver maximum performance. The 440 was a little more "user friendly" and – at no extra charge in the GTX – a lot cheaper.

■ *The GTX did not have real attention-grabbing styling. The cars had many gimmicks to try to boost sales. They included non-functional simulated hood scoops, stripes and badges.*

■ *The GTX never wavered from its role of high-content muscle car with a nice assortment of big-block power. It shared the Belvedere body – including special high-performance hood – with the Road Runner.*

■ *The GTX and other Mopar performance models came with "sticky" F70-14 Goodyear tires. White Streak or Red Streak styles were standard, but raised white letters were catching on at this time.*

That the Belvedere GTX should have been one of the most popular muscle machines is a given. It was good looking, good and fast and a good bargain. That the Belvedere missed the mark in sales is now in the history books. The stripped-down taxi-cab-like *Road Runner* is the car that sold like hot cakes. Cheap thrills are what car buyers wanted in 1968.

The Belvedere GTX was not cheap. The concept behind it was of a high-horsepower, high-content muscle car that gave you good value for your money. In many ways, the 440 was the engine best suited for the GTX. For one thing, you could get it with air conditioning, which was not true in the case of the Hemi. For another thing, it was probably more smooth and practical for highway driving. And it gave nearly (but not quite) the same performance for much less money. So, why would anyone want a Hemi GTX?

Either they were already planning to take it to Barrett-Jackson 40 years later or they read the comparison test of a Hemi GTX convertible and a 440 GTX hardtop in *Car Life*, which said it had "never tested a standard passenger car with the accelerative performance of the Plymouth GTX."

The Hemi-powered convertible used in the test also had power steering, power windows, front disc brakes, tinted glass, a center console, a limited-slip differential, a light package, full wheel covers, head restraints and an AM radio, which upped

its window sticker to a hefty $4.874. The Hemi V-8 was linked to the beefed-up TorqueFlite that Plymouth utilized with its big-block engines.

The Hemi carried twin Carter AFBs with 1.44-inch-diameter primaries and 1.89-inch secondaries. It featured mechanical valve lifters, push rods and overhead rocker arms. The dual exhaust system included reverse-flow mufflers, fat 2 ½-inch exhaust pipes and 2 ¼-inch tailpipes. The engine was rated for 425 hp at 5000 rpm and 490 foot-pounds of torque at 4000 rpm. The power to weight ratio worked out as 10.2 pounds per horsepower. You could scat from 0 to 60 mph in 6.3 seconds or do the full quarter mile in 14 seconds at 98.5 mph.

As might be expected, *Car Life* found that the ragtop rattled and squeaked more than the hardtop. In fact, there was much squeakiness in the top to windshield joint. The styling drew high praise, except for the use of fake hood scoops. The interior was described as "one of the best-executed of current safety-oriented layouts." The car had a nice, safe instrument panel layout and exceptional driver visibility. It was noted that convertibles had a different spare tire location than the hardtop. The spare was mounted flat near the rear right corner of the car and this cut down on useable trunk space (On the hardtop the spare was tucked way up near the rear of the back seat.)

As we hinted, the GTX was a rare car in both body styles and with either of the big V-8s. Plymouth built only 17,914 hardtops and 2,026 ragtops. It's believed that around 410 hardtops and 36 convertibles with Hemi engines were made.

PICTURE PERFECT DETAIL:

Plymouth's very slick answer to the Pontiac GTO. Standard 440-CID 375-HP Super Commando V-8 (426-cid 425-hp dual four-barrel Hemi V-8 is $604.75 extra). Heavy-duty suspension. Heavy-duty torsion bars. Heavy-duty anti-sway bars. Foam-padded front bucket seats. Simulated walnut grain door and instrument panel trim. Wall-to-wall carpeting. F70-14 Red Streak or White Streak tires. Body accent stripes. Heavy-duty brakes. 70-ampere battery to help spin the big motors. Roof drip rail moldings and custom body sill moldings to help spin heads. Firm-Ride shock absorbers. Arm rests, ashtrays and dual horns. TorqueFlite automatic transmission.

■ *The 426-cid 425-hp Street Hemi was the most powerful engine fitted to an American production car, even though it wasn't the biggest. The big valve covers used on the Hemi were much larger than the 440 style covers.*

1968 Plymouth Belvedere GTX

51

1969
Plymouth Road Runner 383

From the beginning, the Road Runner hit a resonant note with the growing number of "youth market" buyers.

New grilles and new rear end styling characterized the 1969 Plymouth Road Runner models, which were now available in three different body styles. The original coupe version Model RM21 found 33,743 buyers. The hardtop Model RM23 had 48,549 assemblies. The all-new convertible, Model RM27, was a rarity with only 2,128 of the 3,790-pound ragtops being turned out.

The standard engine for the Road Runner was the 383-cid V-8, which had a 4.250 x 3.375 inch bore and stroke. With a Carter AVS four-barrel carburetor and 10.0:1

■ *Standard technical features of the 1969 Road Runner included a heavy-duty suspension, heavy-duty brakes, heavy-duty shocks, an un-silenced air cleaner and a four-speed manual transmission with a Hurst gear shifter.*

PICTURE PERFECT DETAIL:

Based on the Satellite, the Road Runner also included a heavy-duty suspension system and heavy-duty brakes. There were cartoon-character Road Runner nameplates on the dashboard, deck lid and doors. Top-opening hood scoops were standard. Under them was a base 383-cid 335-hp V-8 dressed-up with a Hemi Orange paint treatment, chrome oil filler cap and un-silenced air cleaner. Fat F70-14 red- or white-streak tires were another part of the car's makeup. The standard walnut-knobbed shifter was a Hurst unit linked to a four-speed manual gearbox. It had a reverse-gear warning light. A deluxe steering wheel was provided in two-door hardtops and convertibles, but not in the super-low-priced ($2,928) coupe.

■ *Road Runner visual hints included dash, door and deck lid nameplates, top-opening hood scoops, chrome engine parts, a Hemi Orange paint treatment, red or white-streak tires and a fake walnut gear shifter knob.*

compression ratio, the Road Runner engine produced 335 hp at 4600 rpm. Engine options included the 440-cid V-8 or the 426-cid Street Hemi.

From the beginning, the Road Runner hit a resonant note with the growing number of "youth market" buyers. It was originally designed as an inexpensive, "sleeper" muscle car with a factory hot-rodded engine in a very plain Belvedere body shell. Only a small Road Runner badge suggested the car's real nature. But when "stripper" muscle car sales died down, Plymouth started changing the formula with flat-black-finished hoods, bright colors and large air scoops.

Car Life magazine noted the above, when it tested a 383-powered Road Runner in its January 1969 issue. The magazine also noted that the car Plymouth public relations supplied wasn't exactly stock. It actually had many of the same modifications that restorers are likely to make today. For instance, an Edelbrock high-rise manifold, a 780-cfm Holley carburetor, a set of tuned-length Hooker headers and a high-performance factory cam.

With the headers capped and with F70-14 Goodyear Wide-Tread street tires, the car turned a 14.7-second quarter mile at 100.4 mph. This compared to a 15.37-second quarter mile at 91.4 mph for a stock '68 Road Runner.

The handling of the '69 Road Runner, with Hemi-type upgrades and modifications, was rated "above average for a supercar" by *Car Life*. The car did exhibit a degree of understeer, but its handling was "predictable." The magazine said it was hard to get testers tired of driving the car.

Power assisted brakes with cast-iron drum brakes were used at the front and rear of the Road Runner, 11 x 3 in. up front and 11 x 2.5 in. in the rear. Unfortunately, the car's braking performance wasn't up to its power or handling. "Neither decelerative force nor fade resistance were acceptable for the (car's) performance potential" said the report. *Car Life* was also critical of the car's four-speed manual gearbox. "The box in our Road Runner was precise and roadworthy," said the tester, "But the synchro balk rings had a mind of their own and it took a stronger arm than ours to make snap shifts."

■ *A new radiator grille and a new rear end design characterized the 1969 Plymouth Road Runner. It was again offered as a two-door "post" coupe and a two-door hardtop, while a convertible model was brand new.*

■ *Road Runner visual hints included dash, door and deck lid nameplates, top-opening hood scoops, chrome engine parts, a Hemi Orange engine paint treatment, red or white-streak tires and a fake walnut gear shifter knob.*

Other troublesome elements of the Road Runner included a "slippery" front bench seat and a tachometer that was too small to read easily. That the car didn't come with the fanciest appointments was a given for this "low-bucks" champion, but someone at Plymouth PR made a major goof by supplying a car with a non-functioning "beep-beep" horn!

Car and Driver magazine featured a Hemi Road Runner coupe in its own January 1969 issue. The Street Hemi V-8 had a 4.25 x 75-inch bore and stroke, plus hemi heads, a 10.25:1 compression ratio and dual four-barrel Carter carbs to considerably boost its output. It did 0-to-60 mph in 5.1 seconds and the quarter mile in 13.54 seconds at 105.14 mph.

■ *The Road Runner came with F70-14 Goodyear tires. 14 x 5.5JK wheels with a 5/4.5 bolt pattern were standard and 15 x 6JJ wheels were an option.*

1971
Plymouth
Hemi 'Cuda
Convertible

If you are looking for the ulitimate Mopar,
look no further than the Hemi 'Cuda.

The Barracuda body that Plymouth introduced in 1970 had its own architecture. Gone were the days of the Barracuda sharing body structure with the small-engine Valiant compact. The Mopar designers had to keep up with the big-block Camaros, Cougars, Firebirds and Mustangs, so a big engine bay that could gulp up a big-block 383, a 440 Six-Pack or the Hemi was an essential part of the car's design process from day one.

To be totally frank, no one needed a Hemi. The less costly engine choices like the 340 small-block V-8 or the entry-level 383 big-block V-8 were enough engine for almost any 'Cuda buyer. Ordering the bigger 440 Wedge or the "King Kong" 426 Hemi meant adding stiff, harsh-riding springs and shocks and other hefty (and hefty-priced) components that weren't really needed – or even easy to appreciate – on rides to the corner grocery store.

■ *The 1971 Plymouth 'Cuda was a low, wide "pony car" that was long on looks. Its engine bay could accommodate any Mopar engine from the Slant Six right up to the "King Kong" 426-cid Street Hemi.*

The problem was that Plymouth couldn't just stuff a Hemi under the hood and sell the car to any buyer or it would have lost lots of lead-footed young drivers unable to control their suicidal tendencies. The entire car had to be "hardened" like Air Force One to deal with the awesome power of the Hemi.

Of course, there was a small group of serious enthusiasts who craved to go faster than anyone else and had the driving talents to handle a car made to fulfill their desire. As *Muscle Car Review* magazine stated it, "If you are looking for the ultimate Mopar, look no further than the Hemi 'Cuda."

The snorty, king-of-the-options-list Hemi dated back to the 1950s, when it turned big Chryslers into Mexican Road Race winners and 300 Letter Car NASCAR champs. One – or more – big "Firepower" Hemis motivated many slingshot dragsters of that era. After the Auto Manufacturers Association clamped down on horsepower, the Hemi disappeared for a while. It returned with a vengeance in the mid-1960s, when companies like Plymouth had to win drag races to sell cars. The Race Hemi came first, followed by the Street Hemi. The '71 Hemi 'Cuda again had the familiar 426 big cubic

■ *The 1971 version of the Street Hemi V-8 had a lower 10.2:1 compression ratio and stuck with the use of a single four-barrel carburetor. Hemi Orange paint set off the chrome engine accents under the hood.*

■ *The Hemi 'Cuda's power was high, but sales of the street racing car were low. Insurance companies disliked Hemis and helped to keep sales down with high premiums that young drivers couldn't afford.*

■ *Full gauges were a good idea for monitoring the Hemi's performance.*

PICTURE PERFECT DETAIL:

Based on the Plymouth Barracuda, the Hemi 'Cuda also had as standard equipment sill moldings, wheel lip moldings and belt moldings, a heavy-duty suspension with stiffer springs and shocks, heavy-duty auto-adjusting drum brakes (front discs optional), special 'Cuda ornamentation, hood hold-down pins, 9,000-candlepower driving lights and a wider front track. The Hemi 'Cuda also came with 15 x 7-in. wheels and 60 percent aspect-ratio (F60-15) tires with raised white letters. An exposed cold-air dome was standard equipment. The base engine was the Mopar 383 four-barrel V-8. Buyers could add the 440 in four-barrel or six-barrel format or go all the way up to the 426-cid Hemi with dual four-barrel carburetors for $883.90 additional cost. The Hemi V-8 was not available with three-speed manual transmission, air conditioning, automatic speed control or a trailer tow package. A 70-amp battery was also standard and came in handy to get the big Hemi going.

1971 Plymouth Hemi 'Cuda

■ The Hemi was not available with the standard three-speed manual transmission. The heavy-duty New Process A-833 four-speed gearbox or TorqueFlite automatic was mandatory with the torque-twisting Hemi.

■ The 'Cuda interior was a handsome-looking package and all of the "muscle car" soft trim goodies like bucket seats, a center console and a floor mounted shifter were there as standard or optional equipment.

■ *Rather than being a modified version of Plymouth's compact Valiant, the final-generation Barracuda was a real pony car that looked more like a Camaro or Mustang. The 'Cuda model was the high-performance version.*

inches and again carried a 425-hp rating. Its compression ratio dropped a bit to 10.2:1. With a single four-barrel carburetor, the Hemi made 490 ft. lbs. of axle-twisting torque at 4000 rpm.

Hemis came attached to either a heavy-duty New Process A-833 four-speed manual gearbox or the 727 TorqueFlite automatic. The standard rear axle was 3.23:1 geared 9-3/4-inch Dana unit kept in place by Plymouth's sturdy S15 leaf-spring rear suspension with six leafs on the right and five leafs, plus two half-leafs, on the left. Sure-Grip-only options included 3.55:1, 3.54:1 and 4.10:1.

The Hemi 'Cuda was fast. It could streak from 0 to 60 mph in 5.8 seconds and consume the quarter mile in 14 sec. at 102 mph. With a front disc/rear drum brake setup, the Hemi could stop well, too.

By the time the 1971 'Cuda model run came to an end, only 108 hardtops had left the factory with a Hemi V-8 below their hood and 60 of them had four-speed manual transmissions. Far more spectacular in terms of rarity were Hemi convertibles. Only seven of them were made and only two had a manual gearbox.

The 'Cuda was fast and furious for the '70s muscle head.

1964
Ford
Galaxie
Convertible
427 Dual-Quad
R-Code

The 427 was the hot ticket for

stock car stocking.

With "performance" as their byword in 1964, the '64 Fords had a ready-to-go-fast look. New body styling with a strong, lavish use of sculptured sheet metal from stem to stern helped the gorgeous Galaxie achieve a racy appearance.

A full-width horizontal-bar grille with triple vertical ridges and wide-spaced side-by-side headlights gave the Galaxie a "customized" image. The rear deck lid latch panel

■ *Galaxie 500/XLs included shell-type bucket seats, a console, a floor shifter, polished door trim panels, dual-lens courtesy/warning lights in the doors, rear reading lights in hardtops and Galaxie 500/XL badges.*

■ *Convertibles in the Galaxie 500 and Galaxie 500/XL lines got a new type of back window for 1964. It was made of pliant, 0.080-inch-thick tempered glass and was not supposed to scratch or discolor.*

was deeply scooped to surround Ford's trademark large, round taillights. On the plush Galaxie 500/XL it housed a horizontal silver anodized beauty panel. This top-of-the-line model came only in hardtop and convertible models and the two-door versions were sometimes converted into muscle cars with standard bucket seats, a center console and optional 427-cid V-8s.

The highly successful 427 was available in three versions, which were reviewed in great detail in the March 1964 issue of *Car Life* magazine. All three engines were fairly costly. The Q-code 427-cid 425-hp engine cost $461.60, plus $109 for a dual-carb setup. It was the volume-production version of the 427 that most showroom buyers ordered. Ford expected to make 10,000 to 15,000 of these. This 427 "street" engine had a 10.7:1 compression ratio and used normal premium gas, although super-premium was recommended. It had cross-bolted mains, a cast crankshaft and slightly-looser-than-normal fitting pistons.

Carrying the same advertised horsepower rating as the first engine, the 427-R developed more torque. It carried two four-barrel carburetors on a special intake manifold and had revised-port heads and a cam with slightly more overlap than normal. Although this V-8 could be dealer ordered, it was not a street motor.

Designed for racing, the last 427 was a not-for-public-sale NASCAR version. To meet racing rules it had a single four-barrel carb. The block was custom milled and fitted with special cylinder heads, a high-rise intake, a NASCAR camshaft, special high-strength-alloy bearing caps and other unique features. Stronger push rods, a special air intake chamber and a baffled, high-capacity oil pan were used. *Car Life* estimated output at 520 hp at 6500 rpm.

■ *Interiors for the Galaxie 500/XL showed the opulence of Ford's top-of-the-line flagship model. A center console, floor shifter and thin-shell front bucket seats were standard equipment for the XL.*

■ *A rear view of the Galaxie 500/XL shows the anodized trim plate stretching between the traditional big, round Ford taillights. Dual exhaust were part of the 427 package.*

A four-speed manual transmission was standard in Fords with a 427. A special heavy-duty automatic transmission was developed as an option for use with high-output 427s like the R-code version. It actually consisted of a Lincoln gearbox behind a Ford Cruise-O-Matic torque converter with a special aluminum housing. A small number of special parts were added to the transmission to help handle the extra torque. Actual in-the-car performance for this tranny was about equal to that of a good four-speed manual gearbox, but more consistent.

The 427-powered full-sized Fords were the hot ticket for stock car racing and to get them sanctioned for NASCAR, Ford kept making big muscle cars. A high-rise manifold and "high-rev" package were certified as production options and were

also legal for racing. A Galaxie A/Stock dragster package was offered for two-door 427-powered models, as was a B/Stock Dragster package (which added a low-riser manifold). These cars came in white with red interiors. Body sealer, sound deadening insulation and heaters were deleted. Added were lightweight seats and a fiberglass "power bubble" hood. The grilles were modified with fiberglass air induction vents. These packages didn't make sense for heavier convertibles.

Motor Trend described the '64 Fords as big, solid cars that do what they're supposed to and very well indeed. "From the accessory-loaded family sedan to the fierce drag-strip contender, all show the results of Ford's Total Performance package," said assistant technical editor Bob McVay. "And on some Fords, the Total is more total than on others." A 427-powered stock-bodied Ford was basically good for a 0-to-60 time of just over six seconds and a quarter-mile time of just under 15 seconds.

PICTURE PERFECT DETAIL:

Deluxe wheel covers. Thin-shell front bucket seats. Console. The R-Code "Thunderbird Super High-Performance" engine carried two large Holley carbs to help boost output to 425 hp at 6000 rpm. The Super High-Performance package included a heavy-duty suspension and battery, a 40-amp. alternator, a chrome engine dress-up kit, 6.70 x 15 four-ply nylon tires and powerful, fade-resistant brakes. All 427-R cars with automatic transmission used a special heavy-duty Cruise-O-Matic with a 2100 rpm stall speed and 2.1:1 multiplication.

■ *Motor Trend* tested a Galaxie 500/XL with the 427 R-Code V-8 and four-speed manual transmission in its February 1964 issue. The car smoked its rear tires and did the quarter mile in 15.4 seconds at 95 mph.

1964 Ford Galaxie

1965
Ford Galaxie
Hardtop
427 Dual-Quad
R-Code

"There's something satisfying and confidence inspiring about a car that does not lurch and sway over normal highway undulations," *Car Life* said.

A massive horizontal front end set off by a grille featuring horizontal bars and vertically-stacked headlights at each end was among the styling changes for the 1965 Ford Galaxie 500/XL. At the rear were new "squared oval" taillights that broke with Ford's round-taillight tradition. There was generally a bit less bright metal trim and ornamentation on big Fords than in previous years, since the "clean look" was in with Detroit. Two-door hardtops retained a semi-fastback roof and sculptured accent lines again accentuated the body side sheet metal.

■ *It's likely that the majority of full-sized Fords fitted with the 427 (except for all-out race cars) were Galaxie 500/XLs. This car has a special "bubble hood" designed for drag racing applications.*

■ *Full-size '65 Fords were billed as "the newest since 1949." The Galaxie 500/XL series emphasized luxury, but offered several high-performance engine options. This was the first year for a coil spring rear suspension.*

When it tested the Ford 427 Galaxie 500/XL two-door hardtop with dual four-barrel carburetors in its February 1965 issue, *Car Life* magazine described it as "a veritable draft horse of a car" and acknowledged that it was "tailored to the tastes of the knowledgeable and muscular." That meant that test car had a heavy-duty suspension, a stiff clutch, a sturdy four-speed manual gearbox, a high-performance rear axle and no availability of power steering or power brakes.

The testers found the car to be "clumsy and muscle-bound awkward," but clarified that it was "outstanding at moving a heavy load at an impressive rate of acceleration." More specifically, the 4,426-pounds Sport Coupe achieved 60 mph from a standing start in just 4.8 measly seconds and devoured the quarter mile in 14.9 seconds at 97 mph. Which shows what a car with a 10.4-lb./hp power-to-weight ratio can do.

Driving the Galaxie 500/XL two-door hardtop on the then-new Carlsbad Raceway drag strip, in Carlsbad, California, took some doing, which *Car Life* described in minute detail. Too much throttle would make the 8.15 x 15 four-ply nylon tires smoke, rather than bite into the asphalt. Not enough throttle caused the engine to stumble at low rpms and delay blast off. The proper technique was to feather the clutch in, when the tach was reading in the 3500-4000 rpm range, which then fed a gentle flow of power to the rear wheels. At that point, the Ford would come "scrabbling off the starting line like a Super/Stock champion." This would normally result in consistent under-15-second drag strip runs.

■ *A Ford Galaxie 500XL two-door hardtop with the 427-cid 425-hp Thunderbird Super High-Performance V-8 could be purchased for as little as $3,233 in 1965. Car Life's test car ran $4,275 with its optional equipment.*

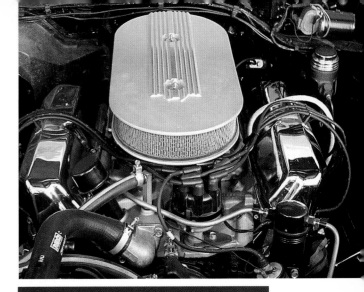

On the highway, the 427 Galaxie showed its true high-speed character in a recorded 0 to 120-mph time of 30.5 seconds. Without power steering or power brakes (both of which were not available with 427s) the car steered too slowly to be considered a real "sports car." The standard heavy-duty suspension was good, but it also altered the big Ford's front-to-rear weight balance to 55.3/44.7 percent, which had a bit of a negative effect on vehicle control at high speeds.

On the other hand, the mandatory heavy-duty brakes increased stopping performance and increased fade resistance. It took the testers four panic stops to induce any fade at all. While 427s had the same basic chassis as other full-size Fords, they came with heftier 0.88-inch diameter front anti-roll bars, stiffer rear coil springs and beefy, specially calibrated shock absorbers. "There's something satisfying and confidence inspiring about a car that does not lurch and sway over normal highway undulations," *Car Life* said.

Strangely enough, the 427 Galaxies came with the same "idiot lights" engine-monitoring devices as other big Fords, rather than full instrumentation. *Car Life* felt that this factor, as well as the lack of some creature comforts and power options reduced the 427 Galaxies' appeal as an "executive's hot rod." While that may have been the case, the "CEO of drag racing activities" wasn't complaining a bit. With consistent under-15-second passes, the 427 Galaxie was a force to be reckoned with.

PICTURE PERFECT DETAIL:

Clean, sharp, square lines characterized the fresh body styling. Special interior upholstery and trim. Deluxe type wheel covers. Thin-shell front bucket seats. Center console. Floor shifter. R-Code "Thunderbird Super High-Performance" V-8 engine with cross-bolted main bearing caps, impact extrusion pistons, special connecting rods, header-like exhaust manifolding, a special camshaft and a special valve train design ($461.60). Dual extra-large Holley carbs ($109). Super High-Performance package including heavy-duty suspension and battery, 40-amp. alternator, chrome engine dress-up kit, 8.15 x 15 four-ply nylon tires and powerful, fade-resistant manual brakes. All 427-R cars with automatic transmission used a special heavy-duty Cruise-O-Matic unit with a 2100-rpm stall speed and 2.1:1 torque multiplication.

■ *The Galaxie 500/XL featured bucket seats, a floor shifter, polished door trim panels with lower carpeting, dual-lens courtesy/warning lights, rear reading lights in hardtops, Galaxie 500/XL badges and deluxe wheel covers.*

1965 Ford Galaxie

1967
Ford Fairlane 500/XL

Hardtop 427 Dual-Quad R-Code

Unlike the earlier racing-only Fairlane Thunderbolts, these later 427 Fairlanes were hot street machines.

To counter GM's tire-shredding GTOs, 4-4-2s, Grand Sports and SS 396s, as well as Chrysler's "Street Hemi" powered Mopar intermediates, Ford Motor Company produced a limited number of 427-powered Fairlane 500 and Fairlane 500/XL hardtops and coupes. These cars easily accommodated the 427 big-block V-8 in both single- and dual-four-barrel configurations. Both engine options were backed up by Ford's tough "Top-Loader" four-speed gearbox.

■ *Ford engineers knew that the near-the-front hood scoop used on Mercury Comets was an effective design, so they placed the hood scoop inlets on 427 cars in that same vicinity.*

Unlike the earlier racing-only Fairlane Thunderbolts, these later 427 Fairlanes were hot street machines. Enthusiasts could buy these "machines" right off the showroom floor at their local Ford dealership.

Ford had introduced an all-new Fairlane body in 1966 and everyone in the muscle car world knew it was designed to compete head-to-head with the Pontiac GTO, which was then "King" of the mid-size muscle cars. It even resembled the "Goat" with its rectangular "Coke-bottle" look and vertically stacked headlights in its front fenders.

For 1967, the Fairlane continued using this same good-looking body, with only the smallest changes in trim and ornamentation. The 1967 grille was made with a single aluminum stamping, instead of the two-grille design used in the previous model.

■ *The '67 Fairlane used the body introduced in 1966 with minor changes. The new grille was a single aluminum stamping, instead of the two grilles used previously. The back-up light divided the taillights horizontally.*

Maybe the "split" grille of 1966 was just too GTO-like! The new 1967 taillights were divided horizontally by the back-up lights, instead of being divided vertically, as they had been in 1966.

For those who wanted to order out a really brutal muscle car, the famous 427-cid "side-oiler" V-8 was again available on the Fairlane options list. For those who wanted a real "stripper" style drag racing car, the big-block Ford engine could be added to the base Fairlane Club Coupe. If you ordered the 425-hp version with two four-barrel carburetors, what you essentially got was a cheap $2,200 mid-size car with an $1,100

■ *The Fairlane 500/XL was Ford's most luxurious intermediate, but to maintain the Total Performance image, these cars were offered with the high-performance 427-cid V-8 in 410- and 425-hp versions.*

big-car engine option. In other words, you could get a true drag racing car from your local Ford dealer for as little as $3,300.

The big engine actually came in two different versions and both of them could also be had in the fancier Fairlane 500 Club Coupe, the Fairlane 500 two-door hardtop or the Fairlane 500/XL two-door hardtop. Officially, no 427 was available in any convertible in any series or in any Fairlane GT model.

The milder 410-hp single-four-barrel-carburetor version of the 427 was the first choice. It had a single four-barrel carburetor. Then came the "hairier" 425-hp version that carried two four-barrel Holleys. Both of these options included a transistorized ignition system, a heavy-duty battery, a heavy-duty suspension, an extra cooling

■ *When you ordered the 425-hp 427 with two four-barrel carburetors, what you essentially got was a cheap $2,200 car with an expensive $1,100 big-car engine option. You could leave the dealer and go racing.*

■ *New for 1967 was the advent of tunnel port cylinder heads for the Ford 427 V-8. The new heads boosted horsepower on cars so equipped by more than 30. The tunnel port V-8s were supposed to be race-only options.*

package and a four-speed manual transmission. A heavy-duty version of Cruise-O-Matic automatic transmission was $220.17 extra.

Also mandatory on Fairlane 427s, at $46.53 additional cost, were 8.15 x 15 four-ply-rated black nylon tires. Buyers could opt for 8.15 x 15 four-ply-rated white sidewall nylon tires for $82.83 extra or for larger 8.45 x 15 four-ply-rated nylon tires. These were available in black sidewall ($62.22 extra) and white sidewall ($98.52 extra) choices.

Racing versions of the 427-cid V-8 were offered with goodies like an eight-barrel induction system that put about 30 extra horses on tap. A tunnel-port version of the 427 was available as an over-the-counter kit, with a tunnel-port intake on special cylinder heads and a special intake manifold.

In NASCAR competition, the 427-powered Fairlanes swept a bunch of early in the year races before Chrysler complained. The sanctioning rules were then changed to handicap the midsize Fords. Similarly, NHRA placed the Fairlane 427s in SS/B class to keep them from totally dominating the quarter-mile sport.

PICTURE PERFECT DETAIL:

All standard Ford Motor Company safety and anti-pollution items. Simulated wood door paneling. Floor carpeting. An electric clock. A "floating" inside rearview mirror mounted on the windshield. Individually adjustable front bucket seats. A center console. A floor shifter. Courtesy door lights. Full wheel covers. A choice of seven all-vinyl interior trims. The 427-cid 425-hp Eight-Barrel V-8 engine. A special hood with a large air scoop on its leading edge. A transistorized ignition system. A heavy-duty battery. A heavy-duty suspension system. Five 8.15 x 15 four-ply-rated nylon tires An Extra-Cooling package. Power front disc brakes. F70-14 Wide-Oval white sidewall tires. A four-speed manual transmission or optional heavy-duty Cruise-O-Matic automatic transmission.

1967 Ford Fairlane 500/XL

1969
Ford Mustang Boss 302
Sports Roof Hardtop

The Boss 302 was Ford's answer to the Camaro Z/28 and was as affordable as it was hot.

I n 1969, Ford reached the peak of its performance years with an array of engines and speed packages the likes of which Detroit is unlikely to offer again. No less than nine V-8s were available, including the awesome Boss 302.

The Mustang's proliferation of '69 models was GM-like and probably followed the thinking of "Bunkie" Knudsen, who became president of Ford after resigning as a GM executive vice-president. Knudsen was famous for turning the Pontiac into a high-performance "youth market" car.

Knudsen hired designer Larry Shinoda away from GM and turned him loose to create some great cars. Knudsen was fond of the fastback body style and made it the basis for a series of hot-performing "buzz bombs" like the racing-inspired '69 Boss 302.

■ *The Boss 302 was Ford's Camaro Z/28 and was likely to wind up in the hands of a hard-working kid or a middle-to-upper income youth wanting a little excitement in his life.*

■ *Popular options on the Boss 302 included a functional, adjustable rear spoiler for $19.48 and Sport Slats with functional rear window louvers for $128.28. Our yellow feature car is the world's best original Boss 302.*

Its hot "Cleveland" heads were also used on Ford's 351 "Cleveland" V-8.

The Boss 302 and other '69 models shared the traditional 108-inch Mustang wheelbase, but overall length grew by 3.8 inches. The Mustang profile was sleeker than ever, thanks to touches like a more steeply raked windshield. Dual round headlights were used for the first and only time on a production Mustang. The outer lenses were deeply recessed into the fender openings, while the inboard units were set into the grille ends.

The indented scoop that had visually "pinched" the Mustang's waist since 1965 was missing from the 1969 design. Instead, a feature line ran from the tip of the front fender to just behind the rear door seam. On the fastback "SportsRoof" models, a backwards C-shaped scoop sat just in front of the rear wheel openings. The '69s had a 0.9-inch lower roofline than earlier fastbacks and a small rear window was new.

The Boss 302 was Ford's answer to the Camaro Z/28 and was as affordable as it was hot. Any grocery boy working at the local supermarket could have saved his weekly paychecks to buy one of these cars. Although the Boss 302 included a hot engine, it wasn't quite as pricey as a big-block V-8. On the other hand, driving it was nearly as exciting as tooling around in a Cobra-Jet Mustang.

What made the Boss special was its beefed-up small-block V-8. Ford engineers fitted the 302 with four-bolt main bearing caps, a stronger crankshaft and redesigned

"Cleveland" cylinder heads that were configured to enhance breathing. In strictly showroom tune, a Boss 302 could turn in 0-to-60-mph times of under seven seconds and nudge the century mark in a standing start quarter-mile. Ford even added an rpm limiter to the Boss 302 to keep lead-footed types from blowing up the high-output small block. Basically, the limiter worked by counting ignition impulses and not allowing the engine to exceed 6,000 rpm.

Besides the special small-block engine, the Boss 302 model can be recognized by a number of distinctive features. The cars had matte black finish on the surfaces of the hood and trunk lid, "Boss 302" name graphics on the body sides, a front-end spoiler and styled steel wheels.

As far as mechanical upgrades to go with the hot engine, Boss 302 standard equipment included front disc brakes and a four-speed manual transmission. A rear spoiler was a popular option available at extra cost.

Unlike many other muscle cars of its era, the Boss 302 had exceptionally good manners when driven on the street. About the only "harsh" aspect of the car was its firm suspension, which let passengers know when pavement irregularities were rolled over.

Inside, the Boss interior was the same as that of regular Mustangs. The interior looked attractive, but it included the infamous Mustang "park bench" rear seat, which was really designed only for munchkins and Lilliputians.

PICTURE PERFECT DETAIL:

Black hood. Black headlight casting. Black rear deck lid. Black lower panel. Four F60 x 15 belted black sidewall tires with raised white letters on 15 x 7-inch five-bolt Magnum 500 argent-painted styled-steel wheels. "C" stripes. Dual exhausts. 16:1 quick-ratio steering. Special handling suspension, including staggered rear shock absorbers. Special cooling package. Non-locking 3.5:1 rear axle. Electronic rpm limiter. Functional front spoiler (shipped knocked down). 45-amp battery. (Power disc brakes and wide-ratio four-speed manual transmission required at additional cost; close-ratio four-speed manual transmission optional).

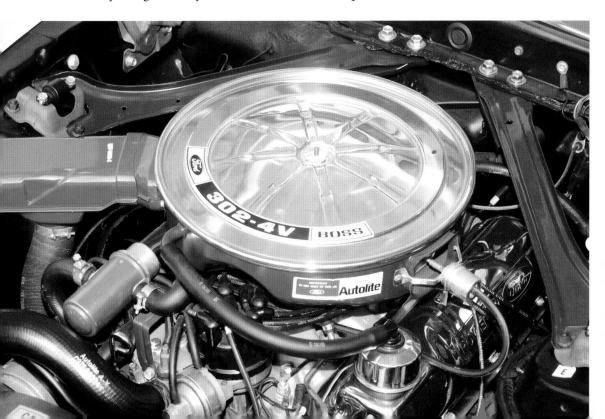

■ *The Boss 302 was a small-block V-8 with four-bolt mains, a beefed up crank and "Cleveland" heads that promoted dramatically better breathing. Engines are "air pumps" and good breathing increases performance.*

1969 Ford Mustang Boss 302

1969
Ford
Mustang
428 SCJ
Sport Coupe

The 428 Cobra-Jet engine
was the fastest running purestock
in the history of man.

Ford's designers went back to their drawing boards to create the Gen III
Mustang. While it had enough traditional touches for people to easily
recognize it as a relative of the first pony car, the '69 also changed quite a
bit at the same time.

■ *The 428 CJ/SCJ was an April 1, 1969, addition to the lineup. Its 335-hp rating was
extremely conservative. Though based on a standard 428, it had special heads and
bottom-end goodies.*

■ *In 1969, Ford claimed to have a "corner on performance." The 428 CJ/SCJ option was available in all models and body styles except the Boss 302 and the Grande Hardtop.*

For one thing, the Mustang gained 3.8 inches of overall length, although it managed to keep the former (and original) 108-inch wheelbase. The windshield had more of a slope to it and there were now four headlights. Two were located in the fender ends and two were tucked into the outboard corners of the grille. Writer Eric Dahlquist accused the new Mustang SportsRoof (fastback) of looking like the GT-40 racing car that made LeMans history. The Sport Coupe probably looked a bit more like the original pony.

Ford added the powerful 428 Cobra-Jet and Super-Cobra-Jet V-8s on April 1, 1968. The former was $287.53 on most Mustangs and a tad less expensive for Mach 1s. The price of the Super-Cobra-Jet version was$357.46 in a Mach 1 and $420.96 in other models. The engines carried a very conservative advertised horsepower rating of 335 hp in both formats, although the SCJ motor actually produced 375 to 400 gross horsepower.

The addition of the 428 CJ/SCJ options to the Mustang offerings reflected the cubic-inch race going on in Detroit at the timer. The options were certainly inspired by big-block V-8s like the Chevy Turbo-Jet 396, the Pontiac 400 H.O. and the Mopar 440 Magnum.

Ford's basic Ram Air 428-cid V-8 had more cubic inches than the legendary 427 "Side Oiler" racing engine, but it was nowhere near as hot. It did, however, get a lot more tepid when special Cobra-Jet heads were added. These cylinder heads resembled the Ford 427's "low-riser" type heads with bigger ports. The CJ/SCJ engines also got the camshaft from the 390-cid GT engine, plus a cast iron replica of the 428-cid Police Interceptor engine's aluminum intake manifold and a huge 735-cfm Holley four-barrel carburetor.

■ *Mustang hardtops had a new cowl vent arrangement that coupled with the heater/blower to funnel cool air out of two adjustable registers above the radio.*

PICTURE PERFECT DETAIL:

428-cid 335-hp four-barrel V-8. Ram Air induction. 80-amp heavy-duty battery. 55-amp heavy-duty alternator. Dual exhausts. Extra cooling package. Bright engine dress-up kit with cast-aluminum rocker arm covers. Functional hood scoop. Cruise-O-Matic transmission or a close-ratio four-speed manual gearbox was required (at extra cost). F70 x 14 Wide-Oval belted white sidewall tires were also required. The Traction-Lok differential with a 3.91:1 or 4.30:1 high-ratio axle was a third additional-cost requirement.

■ *So you think your '69 Mustang 428 SCJ gets better fuel economy than your '69 Mustang 302? Better check your gas receipts. Ford increased fuel tank capacity to 20 gallons from 17, so the cars went further per fill up.*

All Cobra-Jet Mustangs carried Ford's racing-type "R" engine code as the fifth symbol in their vehicle identification number (VIN). They all featured Ram Air induction with a special air cleaner and flapper assembly mounted underneath the hood. A small scoop on top of the hood directed cold air to the single, Holley four-barrel carburetor.

The 428 Super-Cobra-Jet (SCJ) Mustangs were made for enthusiasts to take drag racing. Ford left the top end of the engine alone but beefed up the bottom end and added an oil cooler. The beefing up of the bottom end included a hardened cast-steel crankshaft, externally balanced LeMans connecting rods and an oversize vibration damper. Fortunately, the CJ/SCJ package already included a beefy, nodular-cased nine-inch differential and 31-spline axles.

SCJ motors were coded like CJ motors and both carried the same advertised horsepower rating. The SCJ, however, was the stronger racing mill and certain options

were mandatory to make sure the Mustang could deal with all the power. Either a 3.9:1 Traction-Lok (code V) or 4.30:1 Detroit Locker (code W) axle was required.

Ford's 1969 *Performance Buyer's Guide* described the 428 CJ as "the standard Cobra engine." On paper, at least, it was rated for 335 hp at 5200 rpm and 440 pounds-feet of torque at 3400 rpm. The SCJ – the same engine with Ram Air induction – also had 335 advertised horsepower. It could do 0-to-60 mph in 5.5 seconds and cover the quarter-mile in 13.9 seconds. The estimated top speed of a 428 SCJ Mustang was 115 mph. Expert Alex Gabbard says, "The 428 Cobra Jet engine was the fastest running pure stock in the history of man."

■ *With the larger 1969 body, the capacity of the Sport Coupe's trunk was increased by a whopping 13 percent, which added up to 1.1 cubic feet of enough extra space to carry an additional suitcase.*

1969 Ford Mustang 428 SCJ

1969
Ford
Talladega

Early racing versions of the Talladega
were fitted with the awesome 427
"Side-Oiler" racing engine.

A one-year-only mid-size Ford modle, the sleek and slippery '69 Torino
Talladega was christened after the NASCAR superspeedway of the same
name in Alabama. The car was designed for racing and, under 1969
NASCAR rules, Ford had to make a minimum amount for public consumption.
Producing 500 units was enough to qualify it as a "stock" car. Due to its winning ways
on the superspeedways, the Talladega proved more popular than expected and a total
of 754 were built and came in Wimbledon White, Royal Maroon and Presidential
Blue. All of the cars were built in January and February 1969 at the Ford assembly
plant in Atlanta, Georgia.

■ *The fastbacks competing in the '69-'70 "Aero Wars" on NASCAR tracks were not the
worshipped idols of today. To "legalize" them for racing, 500 had to be built. Ford pinned
its hopes on a sloped-nosed Torino.*

■ *Racing Talladega came with a 429-cid "Semi-Hemi" V-8 that produced over 375 hp. The street versions had the 428-cid 335-hp V-8. They were good for 7.1 seconds zero-to-60 and a 14.7-second drag at 96 mph.*

Ford wanted stock car drivers, not street racers, to create the Torino Talladega's performance image.

There were no options for the Torino Talladega, other than color choice. Each started with a Torino SportsRoof body. To enhance the car's on-track aerodynamics, race car builders Holman & Moody were contracted to craft a special tapering aero-type nose. The front end was extended by five inches and fitted this nose piece and a flush-mounted grille. A Torino rear bumper was cut and re-shaped to fit the front end in a flusher fashion. The rocker panels were also re-contoured and rolled to bring the cars as close to the ground as NASCAR rules allowed.

All Torino Talladegas built for private-party sale came with the 428 Super-Cobra-Jet version of Ford's "FE" big-block V-8. This motor was rated at 335 hp, although actual output was closer to 450 hp. It had a 10.6:1 compression ratio, a steel crankshaft, beefed-up connecting rods, a big 735-cfm Holley four-barrel carburetor and the $155.45 Ford Drag Pack option. The latter package included the new-for-1969 Traction-Lok differential, a 3.91:1 or 4.30:1 high-ratio axle, an engine oil cooler, cap-screw style connecting rods, a modified crankshaft and a larger flywheel damper.

Underneath the Torino Talladega was a double wishbone front suspension and a rear leaf-spring suspension. Staggered shocks were fitted at the rear to prevent wheel hop. The heavy-duty suspension used stiffer springs and stiffer shocks, plus a thicker front anti-roll bar.

Early racing versions of the Talladega were fitted with the awesome 427 "Side-Oiler" racing engine. Beginning in March 1969, the cars were allowed to use the new 429-cid "semi-hemi" engine or "Boss 429" V-8. In an odd manner, Ford actually got this engine NASCAR-certified separately from the Torino body, by making it a Mustang option instead of a Torino option. Somehow, this worked and the 429 was allowed to run in the NASCAR racing versions.

The idea behind the Talladega was to get the production work over with as quickly as possible and let the racers create a performance image for the Torino series. They did this, too. The Torino Talladega won 29 checkered flags, trampling the Dodge Charger 500 in the process. The Talladega inspired the Dodge Daytona and Plymouth Superbird "winged warriors."

David Pearson won his second straight NASCAR Grand National Championship driving for race team owners Holman and Moody in 1969. The 1969 Talladegas were so adept at racing that drivers found that their 1970 replacements were some five mph slower on the big tracks. As a result, Ford's factory-backed teams ran year-old models at many tracks during the 1970-racing season. After 1970, NASCAR banned all of the "wing" cars.

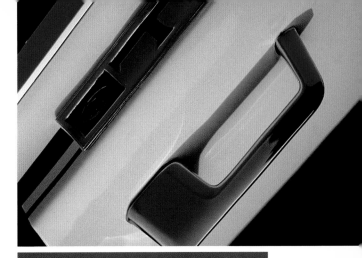

PICTURE PERFECT DETAIL:

428-cid 335-hp four-barrel V-8 with steel crankshaft, beefed-up connecting rods and 735-cfm Holley four-barrel carburetor. Ram Air induction. 80-amp heavy-duty battery. 55-amp heavy-duty alternator. Dual exhausts. Extra cooling package. Bright engine dress-up kit with cast-aluminum rocker arm covers. Cruise-O-Matic transmission. F70 x 14 Wide-Oval belted tires. Traction-Lok differential with a 3.91:1 or 4.30:1 high-ratio rear axle. Choice of Wimbledon White, Royal Maroon or Presidential Blue paint. Tapered aerodynamic nose with five inch extension. Flush-mounted grille. Torino rear bumper cut and re-shaped to make flush-fiting front bumper. Rocker panels re-contoured and rolled to increase lowness. Drag Pack including Traction-Lok differential, a 3.91:1 or 4.30:1 high-ratio axle, an engine oil cooler, cap-screw style connecting rods, a modified crankshaft and a larger flywheel damper. Double wishbone front suspension, Heavy-duty rear leaf-spring suspension. Staggered rear heavy-duty shocks.

■ *Counting prototypes, Talladega production easily passed 500 and hit 754. The cars came in Wimbledon White, Royal Maroon or Presidential Blue with black bench seats.*

1969 Ford Talladega

1966
Mercury Comet Cyclone GT
390 Convertible

Basically, the Cyclone GT was neither a sports car nor racing car, but it was a powerful, sporty ride for everyday transportation use.

T he Cyclone GT was a new-for-1966 version of the mid-size Mercury. The base Cyclone was a plusher version of the Comet that included a 289. You could order an optional 390-cid two-barrel V-8 for $85. If you wanted something hotter than that, you had to add the Cyclone GT package. It retailed for $296.60 and (on paper at least) required that you add a bit for an optional transmission. The package was high in content and was offered only for the sportier body styles like the hardtop and convertible. After all, Mercury didn't want to be building plebian sedans or grocery-getting wagons with racing stripes on them!

■ *A molded fiberglass hood with twin forward-facing air scoops near its front end heralded the arrival of the Cyclone GT at the drag strip. Unfortunately, the non-functional scoops were there only for looks.*

PICTURE PERFECT DETAIL:

Front bucket seats. All-vinyl upholstery. A unique grille. A sports-type steering wheel. Deluxe wheel covers. Floor carpeting. 289-cid V-8. Five 7.35 x 15 black sidewall tires. [Cyclone GT Package] Adds 390-cid four-barrel V-8. Engine dress-up kit. Unique interior and exterior "GT" ornamentation. Dual exhaust system. Floor or console-mounted transmission controls (except column-mounted with three-speed manual or XPL Sport-Shift automatic without Sports Console). Racing stripes above the rocker panels. 7.75-14 Goodyear Power Cushion Wide-Oval nylon white-stripe tires on 5-1/2 x 14-inch diameter wheel rims. Heavy-duty suspension. A 3.265:1 rear axle ratio. Power Booster fan. Twin scoop GT hood made of molded fiberglass instead of stamped steel. Power disc brakes. Extra-cost transmission required.

■ *The Cyclone GT had a five-gauge instrument panel that put all the engine-monitoring dials right in front of the driver, where they belonged. What the gauge cluster lacked, however, was a tachometer.*

The regular Cyclone two-door hardtop and ragtop included bucket front seats, so the GT stuff was really a serious assortment of genuine muscle-car goodies like wide wheels, fat tires, a stiff suspension, a high-speed axle, a Power-Boster fan that drew power only when needed and a floor-mounted gear shifter. Factory literature is a little confusing about the latter point, as it says "optional transmission required," but it also indicates that you could get a three-on-the-tree setup or even automatic on the column if you really wanted to. If you did, we think you also had to delete the 390, as it wouldn't work well with a three-speed stick shift.

As you can see, for all intents and purposes, a four-speed manual gearbox or SportShift automatic transmission was mandatory if you had the Cyclone GT engine. That big-block "FE" family engine featured a 4.054 x 3.78-inch bore and stroke and ran a 10.5:1 compression ratio. Sitting on was a Holley four-barrel with 1.562-inch primaries and secondaries It was rated for 335 hp at 4800 rpm and 427 ft.-lbs. of torque at 3200 rpm. Mark down 6.6 seconds for the 0 to 60 time that Car Life got in its April 1966 road test. The quarter mile took 15.2 seconds with a 90-mph terminal speed.

"Adequate, but not overwhelming," is how *Car Life* summed up the Cyclone GT's drag strip performance. Although Mercury engineers had souped up the engine a bit with a higher-lift cam (raising horsepower from the previous 300) the characteristics of the 390, plus the fact that it carried over 12 pounds per horsepower in the Cyclone convertible, kept a lid on things.

With its unit construction, the Cylone made a pretty sturdy ragtop and Mercury even beefed-up the torque boxes in 1966 for a tighter, quieter ride. The stiff suspension in the muscle model was complemented by fatter steering components. The brake linings were also made of harder material to reduce pedal fade. The Cyclone GT felt a bit front heavy because of its 56/44 weight distribution. "Directional control didn't seem particularly precise," *Car Life* noted. "And the test car was wont to lurch and ramble at highway imperfections."

While its drag strip performance was less than impressive, test drivers enjoyed highway cruising in the Cyclone GT because its trim size made it manueverable. On the flip side, handling on twisting and curvy roads came in for criticism. Basically, the Cyclone GT was neither a sports car or racing car, but it was a powerful, sporty ride for everyday transportation use. It featured good-looking and distinctive styling, a well-thought-out interior with a sporty flavor and plenty of muscle for the average driver who wanted to ride in the fast lane on the Interstate.

■ *Cyclone GT's 390-cid 335-hp four-barrel V-8 was dressed up with chrome-plated rocker covers and a matching oil breather cap. The big Holley carburetor had 1.562-inch primaries and secondaries.*

1970 **Mercury Cougar Eliminator** CJ 428

The big-engine Cougar Eliminator sold for about $3,932 without lots of other factory options.

"**C**ougar Eliminator. Password for action in the '70s," said the headline in the advertisement on back of the October 1969 issue of *Motor Trend*. "Spoilers hold it down and nothing holds it back."

The Eliminator package was raw muscle, straining for the kind of action that muscle maniacs wanted as the new decade began. Little did those hot foots know the horsepower race was soon about to cross its "finish line."

■ *"Cougar Eliminator. Password for action in the '70s," said the bold headline in the advertisement on back of the October 1969 issue of **Motor Trend** magazine. "Spoilers hold it down and nothing holds it back."*

PICTURE PERFECT DETAIL:

The Cougar Eliminator features were a $129.60 option package for both base Cougar and Cougar XR-7 two-door hardtops. The Cobra Jet/Super Cobra Jet 428 four-barrel Ram Air V-8 was the hot engine. The Cougar Eliminator was also available with the standard 351 "Cleveland" V-8 and the optional Boss 302 Trans-Am engine. Eliminator features included hubcaps and trim rings, an all-black grille, flat-black finished hood scoop, front aerodymic "chin" spoiler, raised rear deck lid spoiler with tape stripe, a mid-body "Eliminator" tape stripe in black or silver (in place of the standard Cougar's dual upper paint stripe), "ELIMINATOR" graphics on the rear fender sides, a Rally clock and tachometer. F70-14 raised white-letter tires were required at extra cost. Note: When the Eliminator option was ordered for cars with the 351 V-8, Mercury's Competition Handling Package was required.

■ *The Cobra Jet 428-4V engine was rated for 335hp with or without Ram Air.*

The Eliminator was again based on the standard Cougar, but had a few changes from the '69 model. Six body colors were listed as standard: (M) Pastel Blue, (U) Competition Gold, (D) Competition Yellow, (J) Competition Blue, (Z) Competition Green and (1) Competition Orange. Other colors could be special ordered at extra cost. An upgraded version of the standard Cougar's all-vinyl interior was available.

Exterior details for 1970 included a blacked-out grille with vertical bars that were painted flat black. This type of finish was also used on the bars in the center grille section, which had a completely new design. A large air scoop finished in black sat in the center of the hood. The scoop was functional when mated with the 428 Cobra Jet V-8.

Racing-style outside rear view mirrors were used on both sides of the car, but only the driver's was a remote-control type. There was a flat-black fiberglass front spoiler and a body-color full-width wing-type rear deck lid spoiler (which was decorated with a racing stripe and the Eliminator name).

Four engines were available: the code G Boss 302-cid 290-hp V-8, the code M 351-cid 290-hp V-8 with "Cleveland" heads and a four-barrel carburetor, the code Q 428-cid 335-hp non-Ram-Air Cobra Jet V-8 and the 428-cid 335-hp Super Cobra Jet Ram-Air V-8 (also code Q). The Eliminator package included a 3.25:1 ratio rear axle and F70-14 glass-belted traction tires with raised white lettering. The performance-handling package was required at extra cost on 351-powered Eliminators, but was standard on cars with the other engines.

■ *For 1970 the Cougar Eliminator had a redesigned front end and a new two-spoke steering wheel. Buttons in the spokes operated the horn. Overall length went up 2.3 inches to 196.1 inch.*

The big-engine Cougar Eliminator sold for about $3,932 without lots of other factory options. It weighed approximately 3,321 pounds. The best available information says that 2,267 of the cars were built, of which it is believed that 469 were Boss 302s, 1,424 were 351s and 374 were Cobra Jet/Super Cobra Jet 428s, With the 428-cid 335-hp Super Cobra Jet V-8, the Eliminator was a very fast muscle car. It did 0-to-60 mph in an amazing 5.6 seconds and the quarter-mile took 14.10 seconds at 103 mph.

■ *The "Eliminator" name came from the sport of drag racing, where the big winner was the Top Eliminator who defeated all competitors. The 1970 Cougar Eliminator with the CJ 428 V-8 was a true drag racing machine.*

Desirable Eliminator options included a Traction-Lok differential (3.00:1 or 3.25:1 axle ratio required) for $42.80, a heavy-duty battery for $7.80, power disc brakes for $64.80, an AM/FM stereo radio for $212.50 and styled wheels for $116.60 extra. Ford's Drag-Pack option was available for all Cougars with 428 CJ/SCJ V-8s for $155.50, while the Super Drag-Pack option could be added to Cougars with 428 Cobra Jet/Super Cobra Jet V-8s or the Boss 302 V-8 for $207.30 additional.

In order to add the Ram-Air induction system, the car had to have a 428 CJ option group. Along with the Ram-Air system, the package included a functional hood scoop in body color, hood stripes and a 428 CJ logo for $64.80.

■ *Cougar Eliminators equipped with the 428 CJ/SCJ V-8 featured rear springs that were 16 percent stiffer than stock units. The front springs were the same ones used on other Cougars.*

Mercury Cyclone

Spoiler II

A rare find — the only existing long-nose Cyclone Spoiler II.

When Cale Yarborough drove the Wood Brothers Cyclone to victory in the 1968 Daytona 500, the battle of the "Wing Cars" began. Dodge countered with the Charger 500 for 1969. Ford fought back with the Torino Talladega and Mercury Cyclone Spoiler II. Both featured flush grilles and extended noses.

■ *This rare muscle Mercury belongs to 67-year-old Steve Honnell, of Belfast, Tennessee, who started his drag racing career in 1957. Steve built his first car, a Model T Ford, when he was 11.*

■ *Three-spoke steering wheel carries the Cyclone name at the center.*

■ *The interior of the Cyclone Spoiler II is done in optional Comfort-Weave vinyl in a silver-and-black color combination and includes front bucket seats and a center console.*

The Cyclone Spoiler was a midyear model. At first the main feature was a rear "wing." Originally an aero nose similar to the Talladega's was an option. It finally arrived on the Cyclone Spoiler II. A minimum of 500 of these cars had to be built to qualify them for stock car status and 519 were made. All street versions had a 351-cid four-barrel V-8, not a promised 428-cid SCJ engine. Cyclone Spoilers came in "Dan Gurney" and "Cale Yarborough" editions.

According to muscle-car photographer Jerry Heasley, the car you see here is the only existing long-nose 1970 Cyclone Spoiler II made. Steve Honnell, the owner of a body shop in Belfast, Tennessee, discovered this car in a chicken barn on an Amish farm in Indiana.

The late-Larry Shinoda, who designed such cars, told Honnell that Ford built this car from leftover parts, after the NASCAR program ended. The car was then given to Mose Lane, a Lincoln-Mercury vice president and avid car collector. Lane drove the car on an everyday basis, to work and other places, putting 30,000 miles on the odometer.

Steve Honnell also worked for Lincoln-Mercury in the '60s and '70s. He was a parts and service sales specialist in the company's Atlanta district. Steve was a muscle car enthusiast. He had bought a brand new 1964 Fairlane Thunderbolt. In 1970, he purchased a King Cobra directly from Holman & Moody's NASCAR team. To find out more about the King Cobra, Honnell called Shinoda and started a long friendship. It was Shinoda who told him a 1970 Cyclone Spoiler II had been built for Mose Lane.

Honnell called Shinoda to ask what happened to the Cyclone Spoiler II. He learned that Lane had moved to a farm in Indiana following retirement. Shinoda said Lane apparently still owned the car. It took Honnell five trips to the Hoosier State before locating the farm where Lane had lived. By then it belonged to Amish farmers.

When Honnell arrived at the farm he soon discovered the Cyclone Spoiler II was still in the chicken coop. The roof had fallen in on the car and it was sitting in mud up to the centerline of its tires. Even so, the Mercury was complete and had 30,000 miles showing. Since it was an experimental car, it had no VIN plate and the title, if one ever existed, was long gone. The car was a mess, but it was all there – even the fiberglass front but Ford's 100th Anniversary celebration in Dearborn, Michigan, in 2003.

PICTURE PERFECT DETAIL:

[Cyclone Spoiler II] Competition Orange paint. Extended aerodynamic NASCAR nose cone with removable headlight covers. Fiberglass front bumper painted silver. Adjustable fiberglass rear wing-type spoiler. NASCAR-type Boss 429 V-8 engine with high-nickel-content block, T-rods and solid valve lifters. T & C close-ratio "top loader" four-speed manual transmission with Hurst T-handle shifter. Drag-Pack (including nine-inch rear axle housing, Detroit-Locker differential with 4.57:1 gears and oil cooler behind front grille). Shock absorber towers widened to clear Hemi-type cylinder heads. Bucket seats. Two-tone black-and-silver Comfort-Weave upholstery. Center console. 140-mph speedometer. 8,000-rpm tachometer (mounted in dashboard with optional gauge package). 15 x 7 Magnum 500 wheels. Goodyear F60-15 fiberglass-belted white-letter tires.

■ *Found in an Amish barn, the Cyclone's Boss 429 V-8 provided plenty of horsepower.*

1970 Mercury Cyclone

107

1962 Pontiac Catalina Super-Duty 421 Coupe

By 1960, the "Poncho" performance image had made Pontiac the third-most popular American car nameplate for the first time in history.

"The '62 Pontiac Catalina lightweight sings precious memories from the pre-GTO performance era," Jerry Heasley wrote about the legendary Super-Duty Catalina in the December 1985 issue of *Car Review* magazine. As history tells us, the GTO was John Delorean's successful attempt to sneak a muscle car out to Pontiac dealers after GM issued a ban on high-performance activities in 1963. The Super-Duty Catalina, on the other hand, was a pretty blatant effort by Pontiac Motor Division (PMD) to pull out all stops to build the fastest muscle car on the planet and then use it to blow the doors off its competitor's hottest cars!

■ *An estimate of the original price of a 1962 Catalina Super-Duty 421 two-door sedan is $4,293. The comparable two-door hardtop cost about $4,428. No two Super-Duty cars (or their prices) were exactly alike.*

■ *With a 4.09 x 4.00 inch bore and stroke, the Super-Duty 421 was a huge engine for its day and for Pontiac. Officially it was rated for 405 hp at 5600 rpm and 425 foot-pounds of torque at 4400 rpm.*

PICTURE PERFECT DETAIL:

Extensive use of special made-for-racing aluminum body parts. Special 421-cid 405-hp (500+ actual horsepower) Pontiac V-8 with four-bolt main bearing caps, forged pistons and twin Rochester four-barrel carburetors on a special intake manifold. Borg-Warner T-85 three-speed manual transmission or T-10 four-speed manual gearbox. Lightweight front-end sheet metal (fenders, hood and grille sections). Aluminum rear bumper. Dealer-optional Plexiglas windows. Many Super-Duty Catalinas used a large, functional hood scoop that was actually a Ford truck part that Pontiac purchased in quantity and issued a GM part number for. Optional cast aluminum Tri-Y exhaust headers were added to some cars. It should be noted that not all Pontiac Catalinas that got the 421-cid Super-Duty V-8 engine had factory lightweight body parts.

Back in the 1980s, I went to photograph Dimitri Toth's light blue, '63 Super-Duty Catalina in Pontiac, Michigan. Toth worked for Pontiac and built his car with a personal passion for the company's past racing history. He even got help and some parts from the famous Pontiac engineer "Mac" McKellar. When I photographed the car, it was early on a Sunday morning. Dimitri "lit up" the tires and his neighbors probably thought an earthquake had rocked Pontiac.

PMD was the first automaker to build factory lightweight drag racing cars. This came sometime after it released a number of NASCAR engine options in the early days of 1957. The company had discovered that racing on Sunday sold cars on Monday. The '58 and '59 models added to the Pontiac's transition from an old maid's car to a made-to-go-fast machine.

By 1960, the "Poncho" performance image had made Pontiac the third-most popular American car nameplate for the first time in history. Pontiac went head-to-head with its competition when it released a new engine in 1961. This so-called "Super-Duty" version of the 389-cid Pontiac "mill" served up 368 hp with Tri-Power carburetion. At best, PMD built 25 of these cars.

The Super-Duty 389 was a formidable drag racing competitor, but more power and less weight was the combination needed to keep the Pontiacs winning drag races. So PMD put its lightest, most powerful car on a diet and then a horsepower supplement. Extensive use of aluminum body parts throughout the car and a special 421-cid 405-hp V-8 under the hood created the 3,600-lb. 1962 Super-Duty Catalina.

The new Pontiac 421-cid V-8 featured four-bolt main bearing caps, forged pistons and twin Rochester four-barrel carburetors on a special intake manifold linked to either a Borg-Warner T-85 three-speed manual transmission or a T-10 four-speed manual gear box. Though officially rated at 405 hp, actual output from this massive motor was over 500 hp.

Lightweight parts, in addition to the front-end sheet metal like the fenders, hood and grille sections, included an aluminum back bumper and dealer-optional Plexiglas windows. Many of the Super-Duty Catalinas used a functional hood scoop that was actually a Ford truck part. Pontiac purchased this item in quantity and issued a GM parts number for it. An unusual Super-Duty option was a set of cast aluminum Tri-Y exhaust headers.

Pontiac promotional expert and racing personality Jim Wangers found the 1962 Super-Duty Catalina to his liking. Wangers used such a machine to turn in performances like a 12.38-second quarter mile at 116.23 mph at Detroit Dragway. In all, 225 of the 421-cid motors were built in 1962. They went into 162 cars and 63 engines were made as replacement motors. Not all cars that got the 421-cid Super-Duty engines had factory lightweight body parts.

■ *Super-Duty Catalinas were image cars designed to be seen at drag strips and in race coverage in enthusiast magazines. They were enough like stock Catalinas to help sell lots of look-alike cars.*

1964
Pontiac Tempest LeMans GTO
Sport Coupe
Royal Bobcat

The GTO was not really a model – it was a sneaky option package that Pontiac general manager John Z. DeLorean devised to get a high-performance car on the streets.

In 1963, the Tempest became a "senior" compact and in 1964 it transitioned into a mid-size car with body-on-frame construction. It was this configuration that would become the basis for the world's first "muscle car" – the 1964 GTO.

■ *"GTO—a car for go" stated the cover of **Car Life** magazine in June of 1964. The story inside the magazine said, "A special sort of Pontiac for a special type of customer — the enthusiast."*

■ Twin simulated air scoops decorated the GTO's hood and were used only on Tempest LeMans two-door models with the GTO option. The slender scoop "openings" were at about the midpoint of the hood.

■ The GTO rode on a 115-inch wheelbase and measured 203 inches from bumper to bumper. The coupe weighed 3,106 pounds, the hardtop was 20 pounds heavier and the ragtop weighed the most at 3,360 pounds.

■ *An advertisement for the 1964 Pontiac GTO summed up the character of the first "muscle car" pretty well: "GTO is kicking up the kind of storm that others just talk up!"*

PICTURE PERFECT DETAIL:

[GTO] 389-cid 325-hp V-8 with special camshaft. Special hydraulic valve lifters. 421 H.O. type cylinder heads. Single Carter four-barrel carburetor (Tri-power optional). Specially valved stiff front and rear shock absorbers. Seven-blade 18-inch cooling fan with a cut-off clutch. Dual exhausts. Special six-inch-wide wheel rims. Red-stripe Nylon low-profile tires. GTO medallions. Twin simulated hood scoops. Six GTO emblems. An engine-turned dash insert. Front bucket seats. Special high-rate springs. Longer rear stabilizers. [Royal Bobcat] Thinner head gaskets. Re-curved distributor. Larger carburetor jets. Nylon lock nuts for rockers. Colder spark plugs. Blocked heat rider gasket. Royal Bobcat decals and stickers and "GR-RRR" license plates.

The GTO was not really a model – it was a sneaky option package that Pontiac general manager John Z. DeLorean devised to get a high-performance car on the streets. At that time, GM had a corporate ban on factory use of racing to promote sales. The ban forbade Pontiac to make a 300-cid or larger V-8 standard equipment in a mid-size car.

DeLorean knew he had to do something to keep interest in high-performance alive after racing was banned. The 1964 LeMans could be ordered with an optional 326-cid V-8 that used the same outward size engine block as the 389 big-car engine. A Pontiac engineer who was also a car enthusiast told DeLorean this meant the 389 would fit in the Tempest's engine bay. "Let's try it," said his boss. DeLorean found a loophole that allowed him to market the car. GM rules never said he couldn't make the 389 a LeMans option.

On Delorean's orders, a special GTO was built with an engine put together by Royal Pontiac, a high-performance dealer. This "Super GTO" was given to *Car and*

1964 Pontiac Tempest LeMans GTO

115

Driver to use in a road test. It had a 421-cid Super-Duty V-8 stuffed under its hood and was as fast as a Corvette. However, it looked "factory" and the magazine thought it was testing a stock GTO with a 389 Tri Power V-8.

Fast-forward to 1987, when a GTO fan named Doug McGrew was on his way to the GTO Nats in Wichita, Kansas. McGrew spotted two GTOs for sale in the small town of Meade, Kansas. One was the two-door "post coupe" you see here and the other was a '69 ragtop. Doug noted a low price for both cars and continued on. While at the Nats, he met Milt Schornack, who had worked for Royal Pontiac in '64. Schornack had brought the still-existing 421 Super-Duty GTO magazine car to the event and turned in under-12-second quarter-mile runs with it.

McGrew was very impressed by the car and couldn't forget it. After the Nats, Doug returned to Meade and purchased the two GTOs. He then resold the newer car

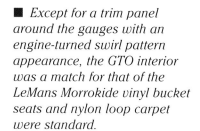

■ *Except for a trim panel around the gauges with an engine-turned swirl pattern appearance, the GTO interior was a match for that of the LeMans Morrokide vinyl bucket seats and nylon loop carpet were standard.*

and kept the '64. McGrew spent five years restoring the coupe. Toward the end of the project, he decided to install a Royal Bobcat kit that he had purchased from Schornack. Doug also added a Mallory electronic ignition and a slightly hotter hydraulic cam to the car's 389.

In January 1964, *Motor Trend* magazine found a GTO-optioned LeMans with the 389 capable of doing the quarter-mile in 15.8 seconds at 93 mph. The same car's 0-to-60-mph performance was 7.7 seconds and it had a 115-mph top speed. With his Royal Bobcat kit and other upgrades, Doug McGrew can make his Poncho go faster than that.

John Z. DeLorean had hoped that Pontiac dealers could sell 5,000 GTOs in 1964. His GM boss, Pete Estes, figured they'd sell more. Estes was right. By the year's end, the GTO was considered a huge sales success. Pontiac records showed production of 7,384 GTO coupes, 18,422 two-door hardtops and 6,644 convertibles.

■ *Included as a part of the base GTO package was a three-speed synchromesh (manual) transmission with a floor-mounted Hurst gear shifter. A four-speed manual gearbox was optional for $188.30.*

1965
Pontiac Tempest LeMans GTO
Tri-Power Convertible

Special advertising promotions were designed to take advantage of the GTO's sales momentum.

The more-successful-than-expected GTO package remained an option for three Tempest LeMans models in 1965. It could once again be ordered for the coupe, the hardtop and the convertible.

This year the car had vertically stacked headlights and the front fenders had small hoods. A new recessed split grille was used. On the GTO, the grille sections were deep set, finished in flat black and decorated with GTO letters on the left-hand side. A redesigned hood had a single central air scoop with two "nostrils."

■ *The 1965 GTO featured a new hood with a single twin-nostril scoop in the center, new front-end sheet metal including a deep-set divided grille and revised taillights with wraparound lenses.*

New taillights were designed to wrap around the rear fenders, essentially creating side marker lights several years before the government required them. The car was three inches longer (206 inches) and a bit heavier. On the inside, things looked mostly the same, but there were new upholstery choices and the instrument cluster had a simulated wood-grain trim panel.

The standard 389-cid GTO V-8 had a four-barrel-carburetor, 10.75:1 compression and 335 hp. All V-8s had new intake manifolds and cams. The 421-style cylinder heads were re-cored to improve the flow of gases. The 335-hp engine was good for 16.1-second quarter mile runs at 89 mph. Its 0 to 60-mph time was 7.2 seconds. For only $115.78 extra buyers could add Tri-Power carburetion with a special 288-degree camshaft that provided 360 hp from the same block.

Stick-shift cars with the Tri-Power engine now used a mechanical progressive linkage, while cars with the Tri-Power V-8 and automatic transmission retained the same vacuum-operated linkage used in 1964. The extra horses went to good use, as the '65 GTO was 340 lb. heavier.

The 335-hp GTO convertible went 0-to-60 mph in 7.2 seconds and did the quarter-mile in 16.1 seconds. Late in the year a 389-cid Ram Air engine with Tri-Power arrived and was put in only about 200 GTOs. It was advertised at 360 hp, but actually had more than that.

Special advertising promotions were designed to take advantage of the GTO's sales momentum. One effort included five huge 26 x 11 1/2-inch full-color photos of the so-called "GeeTO Tiger" in action for only 25 cents, plus a GeeTO Tiger record for 50 cents. The record captured the sounds made as a company test driver put a 1965 GTO through its paces at the GM Proving Ground in Milford, Michigan.

Hurst Performance Products Co., of Glenside, Pennsylvania, sponsored a GTO pace car for *Motor Trend* magazine's Riverside 500 race. Hurst also built a gold colored car with gold wheels to push sales of its popular gear shifters. Amazingly, both of these cars still survive in great condition and the white Riverside 500 car is unrestored.

For 1965, Pontiac Motor Division held the price of the GTO option at $295.90. The package included most of the same items it did in 1964, except that a single dummy hood scoop was used in place of two and the dashboard insert had a wood-grain look rather than an engine turned look.

While sales of the original 1964 model had been held down by autoworker strikes and an abbreviated model year (after the GTO option's midyear introduction), this year Pontiac was ready to open the floodgates. National Sales Manager Frank Bridge thought he could move 50,000 GTOs. He was a bit pessimistic, as the final number was 75,352 units.

The GTO convertible was available for as little as $3,092.90 and 11,311 were made. The GTO coupe had a base price of $2,786.90 and 8,319 assemblies. The sales leader was the GTO two-door hardtop, which could be had for as little as $2,854.90. It was the choice of 55,722 buyers.

■ *On the inside of the '65 GTO, things looked about the same as they did in '64, but there were new upholstery choices. The instrument cluster also had simulated wood-grain trim instead of an engine turned look.*

1969
Pontiac
GTO Judge
Hardtop

All rise...here comes The Judge!

Much has been written about the Judge, but two recent books by men who were there tell the story better. Jim Wangers, who worked for Pontiac's ad agency in 1969, has a full chapter on the Judge in his book *Glory Days: When Horsepower and Passion Ruled Detroit*. Milt Schorrnack, who worked at Royal Pontiac, where the prototype Judge was put together, presents a different perspective in his book, *Milt Schornack and the Royal Bobcat GTOs*.

Wangers worked with John DeLorean and his planning group called the Ad Hoc Committee. Wangers says The Judge was a reaction to the Road Runner. The original idea was to build a cheap, watered-down GTO with a 350 that could beat the Spartan 383-powred Plymouth. DeLorean's reaction – "Don't you know it's a 400-cubic-inch world?" So the gang went back to the drawing board to create the ultimate GTO.

■ *The special Carousel Red color gave The Judge its identity and was the only color available on the car when it first came out. Pontiac even sold a Carousel Red jacket for anyone who wanted to match the car.*

■ *Functional, driver-controlled hood air scoops had Ram Air decals on their sides. There was a blacked out grille and bold, multi-colored "The Judge" front fender decals.*

According to Wangers, DeLorean picked the name for the car, inspired by a popular TV comedy skit.

Wangers mentions a Mint Green GTO Ram Air IV hardtop that Pontiac provided to turn into a Judge prototype. The car was actually developed at Royal Pontiac, the dealership owned by drag racer Ace Wilson in Royal Oak, Michigan. That's where Milt Schornack worked and he talks about that car in his book.

Schornack says the car came into the dealership in October 1968. It had a four-speed and 3.90 gears. He was instructed to tear the car apart and make it into an ultimate GTO. Royal changed everything except the short block. Pontiac wanted The Judge to have standard Ram Air III D port heads with the Ram Air IV's forged pistons. Three different striping treatments were put on the car, which was redone in a new Carousel Red that became a Judge trademark. Schornack says they had to add castor oil to the paint to squirt the Endura bumpers, since no Carousel Red bumper paint was available. This didn't work well, as the paint soon cracked.

The prototype got a Royal Bobcat package, a set of headers and 3.90:1 gearing. It earned its stripes on the street, with Wangers and Royal Pontiac employees driving it.

Pontiac advertised that the Judge was "Born Great." *Car and Driver* called the new option an "econo racer" – a well-loaded muscle car priced to give you a lot for your money. It was a machine that you could take drag racing pretty much "as is" – and win.

Pontiac released the Carousel Red Judge on December 19, 1968. Later, the company added all other GTO colors. The standard production engine was the 366-hp 400 with Ram Air III. A total of 8,491 GTOs and Judges were sold with this motor, including 362 convertibles. The 400-cid 370-hp Ram Air IV engine was installed in 759 cars and 59 were convertibles.

As far as installations of the Judge option went, it was added to 6,725 GTO hardtops and 108 GTO ragtops. The editors of *Car Life* magazine whipped a Judge through the quarter-mile at 14.45 seconds and 97.8 mph. *Supercars Annual* covered the same distance in a Judge with a Turbo Hydra-Matic transmission in 13.99 seconds at 107 mph run!

According to Wangers, The Judge was a car that was perfectly suited to the market in 1969. He feels that its arrogance and wild psychedelic looks made it a hit with the "protest generation" of that time. Unfortunately, there were problems getting the car out of production. "Once the dealers started receiving cars, sales took off like gangbusters," Wangers noted. "Pontiac couldn't build them fast enough."

■ *Many interior options were offered. Power bucket front seats were among them. Buyers could chose a Rally Gauge cluster with Rally clock or a second version with an instrument panel tach.*

1969
Pontiac
Trans Am
Convertible

The car's racing image name was taken from the Sports Car Club of America's Trans-American sedan racing series.

The Firebird name was used on a series of turbine-powered prototypes made in the 1950s. These cars looked like airplanes on four wheels. After the Ford Mustang arrived and took off in sales, GM went to the drawing boards to make its own clones of the "pony car." Pontiac dusted off the old prototype name and called its version of the Mustang-fighter the Firebird. There are photos of a prototype Firebird with one of the old jet cars. The first production Firebird was built at GM's Lordstown, Ohio, assembly plant in early January 1967. Pontiac took the wraps off the car on February 23, 1967, at the Chicago Automobile Show.

Though it was based on the Camaro, the Firebird had many differences from engines to underpinnings. A split grille — which was a trademark Pontiac motif since 1959 — provided a Pontiac identity right up front. Two body styles — coupe and convertible — were offered with many of the same power teams offered in Tempest or GTO models.

■ *All of the 1969 Trans Ams, both Sport Coupes and convertibles, were Cameo White with dark blue racing stripes. Half of the convertibles had automatic transmissions.*

PICTURE PERFECT DETAIL:

Heavy-duty three-speed manual gearbox. Floor-mounted shifter. 3.55:1 rear axle. Fiberglass-belted tires. Heavy-duty shock absorbers. Heavy-duty springs. One-inch stabilizer bar. Power front disc brakes. Variable-ratio power steering. Engine air extractors. Rear deck lid airfoil. Black textured grille. Full-length body stripes. White and blue finish. A leather-covered steering wheel. Special identification decals. RPO L74 400 H.O. V-8 with 335 hp. Note: Certain features listed as "standard equipment" in the first printing of sales literature were not used on production Trans Ams. They included a driver-controlled hood scoop.

■ *Trans Am features included engine air exhaust louvers on sides of fender, a rear deck lid airfoil, a black textured grille, full-length body stripes, white and blue finish, and special decals.*

Firebirds were restyled in late 1968. Design changes included flatter wheel openings, front fender wind splits, new rooflines and a creased lower beltline. The gas filler moved behind the rear license plate and a boxier split bumper grille was used. The headlights were set into square body-colored Endura plastic bezels. The high-performance Trans Am was introduced as a midyear model on March 8, 1969. It was the most highly refined Firebird model-option up to this point.

Standard equipment for Firebirds included vinyl bucket seats, grained dashboards, carpeting, outside mirrors and side marker lamps. The new Trans Am hardtop had a base price of $3,556 and a production run of just 689 units. Only eight convertibles were made. Originally, a ragtop cost only $150 more than a Sport Coupe. The eight cars built were, for many years, the only Trans Am ragtops manufactured.

The car's racing image name was taken from the Sports Car Club of America's Trans-American sedan racing series. Pontiac did have to pay a $5-per-car royalty to the SCCA to use the Trans Am name.

The Trans Am was originally supposed to have a hot 303-cid small-block V-8 that would have met racing rules. In fact, about 25 SCCA racing cars were fitted with this very short-stroke 303-cid tunnel-port V-8. Production versions of the new car, however, were built with either a 335-hp 400 H.O. (a.k.a. Ram Air III) V-8 or an optional 345-hp Ram Air IV engine. All of the 1969 Trans Am convertibles built had the 335-hp motor.

This five-main-bearing, Pontiac-built V-8 used L74 as its regular production option (or RPO) code. Its bore and stroke of 4.125 x 3.746 added up to 400 cid. Pontiac used a 10.75:1 compression ratio. Breathing and fuel mixing was accomplished through a four-barrel carburetor. The 335 hp was developed at 5000 rpm. The engine also cranked up 430 lb.-ft. of torque at 3400 rpm.

Both Firebird body styles used a 108.1-inch wheelbase and had an overall length of 191.1 inches. Overall width was 73.9 inches, overall height was 49.6 inches and the tread, front and rear, was 60 inches. The convertible originally sold for $3,770.

■ *Chief designer Bill Porter was actually against putting stripes on the Trans Am. An early car tested by* **Hot Rod** *did not have them. On some cars, the rear stripes ran under the spoiler; on others they ran over it.*

1970
Pontiac
GTO Judge
Ram Air IV
Convertible

---

*Each dealer had to keep a record of
how his car performed.*

In his book *Glory Days: When Horsepower and Passion Ruled Detroit*, former Pontiac
ad man Jim Wangers outlines how the 1969 GTO Judge was used to reinvent the
GTO as a good class car for amateur drag racing. A small program that worked
through Pontiac dealers was set up. Participating dealers bought a Carousel Red Judge
at normal dealer cost and used it in NHRA drag racing. The dealers got a complete
duplicate drive train free.

Each dealer had to keep a record of how his car performed. If this was done,
Pontiac would supply all replacement parts for the racing car on an exchange basis, for
one year. The program worked well. "Since they all looked alike, it seemed like there

■ *Up front, The Judge included a "chin" type air dam, a blacked-out grille and a 1-1/4-inch
thick stabilizer bar. The twin air scoop hood looked just like the one used in 1969.*

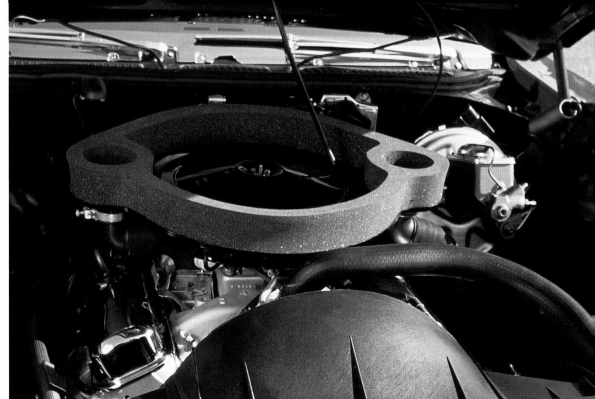

■ *If the 370-hp Ram Air IV V-8 was used in only 37 GTO/GTO Judge convertibles and less than 10 percent of GTOs were Judges, we could estimate that possibly four cars like this one were made.*

PICTURE PERFECT DETAIL:

[GTO] Endura rubber nose. Twin grilles with GTO letters on the left-hand insert. GTO lettering behind front wheel openings. Base 400-cid 350-hp four-barrel V-8. Bucket seats. Vinyl trimmed padded dashboard. Twin air scoop hood. Heavy-duty clutch. Sports type springs and shock absorbers. Carpeting. Lamp group. Dual exhausts. Deluxe steering wheel. Three-speed manual floor shift. Rear suspension sway bar. [Judge] Rally II wheels less trim rings. G70 x 14 fiberglass black sidewall tires. Rear deck air foil. Body side stripes. Judge stripes and decals. Black textured grilles. T-handle shifter on cars with manual gearbox. All regular colors plus special midyear Orbit Orange. Standard 400-cid Ram Air V-8 (400-cid Ram Air IV optional in The Judge at a special price of $389.68, approximately $500 less than in other GTOs).

were many more cars in action," says Wangers. "We didn't care if they never made the lead story in *National Dragster*, as long as they were out every weekend in front of a local crowd."

In 1970, the Pontiac Ad Hoc Committee recommended making the GTO Judge a permanent model that year. Wangers was against this. He considered the wild-looking judge a promotion and he considered the GTO something different – a "serious" muscle car. Since his long-time supporter John Z. DeLorean had left Pontiac for Chevrolet, Wangers was a voice crying in the wilderness and the '70 Judge made the cut.

Pontiac intermediate models, including The Judge, sported new Firebird-like bumper grilles; wraparound front parking lights, wraparound taillights, crease sculptured side styling and body-color nose panels All GTOs added an Endura rubber nose. Twin ovals housed recessed grilles with GTO letters on the left-hand insert. Twin, side-by-side round headlights were recessed in square openings. Rectangular parking lights were under the headlights in a bumper valance that had twin air openings (one on either side of the license plate holder.

At the rear end, wide taillights embedded in the bumper, were narrow and wide enough to stretch around to the center-located license plate recess. The high-performance image car had "The Judge" graphics on its front fenders, behind the wheel openings, as well as on the rear deck lid.

Although the body was heavily revised, the twin air scoop hood was the same as the 1969 hood. The GTO interiors were only slightly changed from 1969. Firestone, Goodyear or U.S. Royal tires, size G70-14 were standard and came in a choice of single- or dual-white-stripe designs.

A base hardtop with "Judge" equipment was about $3,604, or possibly a tad more with mandatory options. Judge convertible prices started at about $3,829. A more powerful Ram Air IV engine was $558 extra. Ram Air IV cars could only be built with either a 3-speed THM or the four-speed manual this car has. Pontiac records show the Ram Air IV V-8 was used in 767 GTO and Judge hardtops and 37 convertibles. Ram Air IV Judge ragtops are very rare.

With the 400-cid 370-hp Ram Air IV engine, a 1970 Judge could do 0 to 60 mph in 5.1 seconds. The quarter mile took 13.9 seconds at 107 mph. No wonder Pontiac promoted the 1970 Judge as "The Humbler." Unfortunately, the promotions fell flat. Judge sales were low. Even the midyear addition of new Orbit Orange paint didn't save the day.

■ *In the middle of the 1970, PMD realized the second Judge wasn't selling and released a new Orbit Orange color as an attempt to approximate the Carousel Red color that helped 1969 Judge sales.*

1962
Chevrolet
Bel Air
"Bubbletop 409"

"She's so fine my 409," the Beach Boys sang.
And man, were they ever right.

Super Stock drag racing became a very popular in 1961. Part of the reason was that the National Hot Rod Association established a dozen different classes for stock-bodied dragsters, usually referred to as "stockers."

Interest in drag racing had grown by leaps and bounds and, with publications like *National Dragster* giving the "stockers" ink, Detroit was suddenly racing again. In 1957, the Auto Manufacturers Association pressured carmakers to stop racing,

■ *Ken Siegfried's 1962 Bel Air 409 "bubbletop" hardtop took first place in the American Muscle and Performance Car class at Meadow Brook in the summer of 2005. It was also selected Good Guys "Muscle Car of the Year."*

■ GM was into "roof innovations" in the late 1950s-early '60s. For example, the "flat-top" sedan of 1959-1960, the convertible-like hardtop of 1962-1964 and the early-Sixties "bubbletop," that came only on Bel Airs in 1962.

■ Police car style over-size black sidewall tires, bare black-painted wheels or painted wheels with "doggie dish" hub caps were common equipment on early high-performance cars like the hot 409 Chevy.

■ *Chevy smoothed out its gull-wing rear end styling for 1962.*

but "backdoor" support of racing continued and it was helping smaller companies like Dodge and Pontiac gain market share. Ford and Chevy executives were forced back into the fray by the stiffening competition.

Transferring the high-performance image created by racing to the showroom products was important. Pontiac's Bonneville had a race-bred name and benefited in sales, even though the lighter Catalina was the real racing car. Ford's sleek Starliner also developed a high-performance following.

In 1961, a total of 456 Chevy Impalas were sold with a $54 Super Sport package that included "SS" emblems, a padded dash, spinner wheel covers, power steering/brakes, heavy-duty springs and shocks, sintered metallic brake linings, a 7,000-rpm tach, 8.00 x 14 whitewall tires, a dashboard grab bar and a chrome four-speed shifter housing. A 409-cid V-8 went into 142 Super Sports.

The big-block 409 was created for use in NASCAR, but Chevy had to sell some to make it "stock." It was available in any model. By the end of the year, the initial 360-hp 409 was joined by a bigger-valve 409-hp job with dual four-barrel carbs. In lighter Bel Airs and Biscaynes, the 409 was a force at drag strips.

PICTURE PERFECT DETAIL:

[Bel Air 409] Dual sun visors. Electric windshield wipers. Heater and defroster. Oil filter. Front foam cushion. Cigarette lighter. Front arm rests. 7.50 x 14 tires. Foam rear seat cushion. Deluxe steering wheel. Glove box compartment light. Carpets. Optional 409-cid 380-hp V-8 including four-barrel carburetor, dual exhausts, high-lift camshaft and mechanical valve lifters or 409-cid 409-hp V-8 including two four-barrel carburetors, dual exhausts, high-lift camshaft and mechanical valve lifters.

1962 Chevrolet Bel Air

137

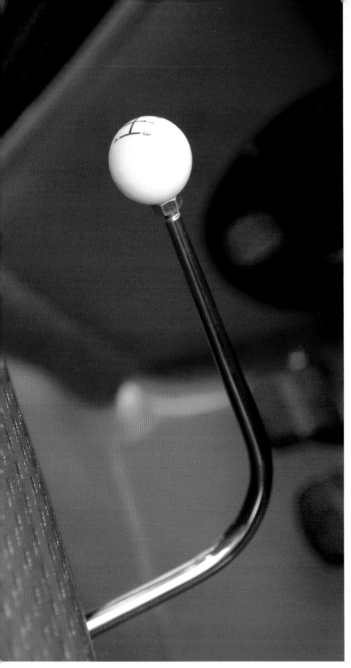

■ *SS trim items did not extrend to door trim.*

■ *Powerglide automatic transmission wasn't available in 409 powered Chevys and Turbo Hydra-Matic automatic transmission wasn't yet available. The T-10 close-ratio four-speed was a mandatory $188.30 option.*

■ *Bel Air Bubbletops tipped the shipping department scales at about 3,360 pounds with a 409 V-8 engine and related goodies. They were actually a better pick for a high performance machine than the Impala or Impala SS.*

The "bubbletop" two-door sedan — Chevy's lightest production model — was the basis of many Chevrolet racing cars. In 1961 you could get a "bubbletop" Impala, but in '62 only the Bel Air series offered it. This heart-stopping body style got its nickname from the vast sweeps of front and rear window glass. Bubbletops weighed about 3,360 pounds with the 409 and related goodies. They were better for racing than the Impala hardtop with its imitation convertible roof.

A 409 was killer fast. The 409 engine could be ordered in about anything Chevrolet built, even station wagons. The exhilarating combination of a 409 in a bubble top was almost too much to imagine. Simply put, a 409 could go. How fast? Try 115 mph at the end of a standing-start quarter-mile. And its power rating? How about 409 hp for the dual four-barrel carburetor version.

"She's so fine my 409," the Beach Boys sang. And man, were they ever right.

■ *The dealer cost of the 409-cid 409-hp big-block engine package was $343 or nearly 10 percent of the total price of a Chevy in 1962. The package, including two four-barrel carbs and other hardware, was $484.65.*

1962 Chevrolet Bel Air

1964
Chevrolet Chevelle L-76

While it's true that the GTO had more low-end torque, the L-76 had more top-end horsepower.

Anticipating a general improvement in the market for cars priced and sized below full-sized models, Chevrolet introduced its all-new Chevelle in the fall as a 1964 model. The Chevelle fit between the compact sized Chevy II and full-size models. Chevelle production was carried out at plants in Baltimore and Kansas City and a brand new factory in Fremont, California.

The Chevelle was styled with square-looking lines and designed in the mold of the Chevy II, but it had curved side window glass. Chevrolet designers put an emphasis on width and a distinctive look. A Super Sport series offered a sport coupe and

■ *The L-76 was intended for drag racing and to compete for muscle buyers with the GTO. Since Chevrolet was in no position to put a big-block into Chevelles, the hot small-block L-76 was used.*

PICTURE PERFECT DETAIL:

"SS"-in-a-chrome-circle badges at the trailing edge of each rear fender and on the right-hand side of the rear body panel. Bright metal mid-body side moldings deleted. Profile moldings from the fender tops to the wheel lips and rocker panels. Five black sidewall tires. Vinyl upholstery. Padded arm rests. Deluxe steering wheel with a horn ring. Back-up lights. Glove compartment light. Electric clock. Carpeting. Front bucket seats upholstered in soft vinyl flanked by bright metal moldings. Sporty center console. Floor mounted gearshift (straight-line shift lever for Powerglide or a stick shift for the four-speed synchromesh). Special engine gauges. Special wheel covers with a radial pattern centered around an exclusive Super Sport emblem, with vented design to allow brake cooling. Optional 327-cid 365-hp L-76 V-8.

■ *Inside the Chevelle SS were front bucket seats upholstered in soft vinyl and trimmed with bright metal moldings. A sporty console was fitted and the floor shift added a sports car feel.*

convertible. These cars had no lower belt trim. Instead, there was a molding running along the full-length of the upper body ridge and continuing along the rear fender edge, plus SS rear fender and rear panel badges and specifically styled wheel covers.

The big-block Super Sport hadn't arrived yet, but that didn't mean that Chevrolet couldn't build a high-performance version of the Chevelle suitable for drag racing. In this era, dropping hot Corvette small-block V-8s into smaller models like the Chevelle was Chevrolet's formula for an instant muscle car.

Though built using this recipe, the 1964 Chevelle L-76 was much rarer than other mid-'60s Chevrolet muscle cars. No exact figure is known for production, but one of the car's features was a specific high-revving tachometer designed and intended for use in these cars. Research by Chevelle experts shows that Delco built only 100 of them. Only a portion of these instruments were used in L-76s, before the program ended. The rest were then used up by making them an El Camino option. So L-76 production was well under 100 units.

When a buyer checked the L-76 option he or she got a special 327-cid 365-hp "Corvette" V-8 featuring the chrome-plated dual-snorkel air cleaner used on the Chevy 409-cid engine, plus a few other minor differences. The classic 2.02-in. cylinder heads were topped by an aluminum intake manifold and a four-barrel Holley carburetor. A K66 Delcotronic full-transistor ignition system was used and required a 42-amp.

alternator. A "30/30" solid lifter cam was used. With an 11.0:1 compression ratio, the L76 V-8 produced 365 hp at 6200 rpm and 350 lbs.-ft. of torque at 4000 rpm.

The L-76 was intended for drag racing and to compete for muscle car buyers with the GTO. Since Chevrolet was in no position to put a big-block V-8 into the Chevelle, the hot small-block L-76 was used instead.

Scott Gaulter spent 10 years gathering authentic parts to build a replica of a 1964-1/2 Chevelle L76, then sold it to Bob Macy. Gaulter's restoration research indicates that all L-76s had a Muncie four-speed manual gearbox. The cars also used a heavy-duty cooling system with a fan shroud with a fan clutch. A telling feature was the 7000-rpm in-dash tach, which indicated engine redline at 6500 rpm. Positraction was another part of the package. Metallic brakes were available and were most likely standard, although Gaulter did not install them.

How does the L-76 Chevelle stack up against the GTO? While it's true that the GTO had more low-end torque, the L-76 had more top-end horsepower. Unfortunately, no car magazine of the era thought of testing the two cars against each other. You just have to wonder if the L76 Chevelle would have won such a race?

■ *When a buyer checked the L-76 option he or she got a special 327-cid 365-hp "Corvette" V-8 featuring the chrome-plated dual-snorkel air cleaner used on the Chevy 409-cid engine.*

1964 Chevrolet Chevelle L-76

Chevy II Nova SS Sport Coupe

327/350 L79 V-8

The L79 Nova SS was actually a mechanical prototype for the Camaro

In 1963, West Coast race tuner Bill Thomas built a Chevy II with a fuel-injected Corvette 327-cid V-8. Later, Thomas made a similar car that combined the Corvette type 327 "fuelie" V-8 with a complete performance kit that included chassis, suspension and braking upgrades. The little car was nicknamed "Bad Bascomb." Thomas' cars got good publicity in all of the important enthusiast magazines and Chevrolet executives paid attention, too. Thomas was showing them what the public

■ *The Nova Sport Coupe had a mild-mannered look, even though its power to weight ratio put it in the muscle car bracket. Though boxy in shape and compact in dimensions, the '66 was a good-looking machine.*

■ *The Super Sport package added glitter to the Nova with its bright body moldings, wide rocker panel underscores, fancy SS wheel discs and rear beauty panel. With its stiff suspension, the L79 sat up tall.*

■ *The heart of the high-performance Nova Super Sport was a 327-cid 350-hp V8 lifted from the Corvette parts bin and tucked under the hood of Chevy's "senior compact."*

wanted and it wasn't a four-cylinder econo car, even though some Chevy IIs came that way.

In 1966, Chevy made a 350-hp carbureted version of the "Corvette" 327 V-8 an option in the Nova SS. With a four-speed manual transmission, posi rear, power steering and brakes, heavy-duty suspension, air conditioning, California emissions, a radio and rear speaker, deluxe bucket seats, deluxe belts, a console, tinted windows and added instrumentation, this car cost $3,662 compared to $2,480 for a base Nova hardtop.

Car Life magazine tested the 350-hp Nova SS in its May 1966 issue and the writer liked it. The 327 was a strong, tractable engine. It gave the Nova a 10.1 lb./hp ratio, which added up to neck-snapping performance. The road test chart showed a 7.2-second 0-to-60 mph run and a 15.1-second quarter mile at 93 mph. "It stands heads above the Supercar level," said *Car Life* of the hot Nova's overall performance. It was pointed out specifically that a 350-hp Nova should be able to hold its own with all Mustangs, except the Shelby GT-350, which was a true racing car. The 350-hp Nova's top speed was 123 mph and did 100 mph in 18.2 seconds.

The L79 Nova was proof that you could have a muscle car without big-block power, if the car was small enough to make a small-block V-8 seem big. The magazine's test driver said that the 327 "provides surprisingly strong punch up to 4000 rpm, all through the lower rpm range where such power plants are normally expected to be lightweight performers." He then tossed in, "Above that point, it's like having another, even larger, engine suddenly switched on."

The test car was powerful, but it was not perfect. Braking hardware and performance was not upgraded sufficiently from what you got with a base six-cylinder Nova. In addition, the steering, though power assisted, was still very slow. *Car Life* also had untypical problems with the Muncie four-speed gearbox and encountered a worn and noisy front stabilizer bar.

The car's upgraded 6.95-15 U.S. Royal Loredo tires (required with the 327-cid 350-hp V-8) exhibited better than average gripping power on wet surfaces and were average on dry pavement. With their larger-than-stock size, the tires actually contributed a bit to handling as well. *Car Life* said that handling of the car was "a cut above competitive." Even with the Nova's single-leaf rear spring layout, the suspension control was well damped and "without vice."

Car Life appreciated the special bucket seats used in the Nova SS, which it described as being "much like those in the deluxe Impala or Caprice." The magazine noted the seats had an exceptionally high back rest, stylish triangular head rests and side bolsters that provided good lateral support.

The L79 Nova SS was actually a mechanical prototype for the soon-to-be-released Camaro (then called "Panther.") After the Camaro's 1967 release, Both cars shared the same front sub-frame and many similar power train options.

PICTURE PERFECT DETAIL:

[Nova SS] Color-accented wide body sill moldings. Front and rear wheel opening moldings with extensions on both lower fenders. Door and rear quarter upper body side moldings. An SS grille emblem. Nova SS rear fender scripts. A full-width ribbed rear deck end panel with a Chevy II nameplate and SS badge. Special 14-inch Super Sport wheel covers. All-vinyl front bucket seats. An SS emblem on the glove box door. [L79] 327-cid 350-hp V-8 with Holley four-barrel carburetor, hydraulic valve lifters and long-duration cam. Four-speed transmission (in Car Life test car). Positraction limited-slip differential. Power steering. Power brakes. Heavy-duty front and rear suspensions with stiffer spring rates and 0.87-inch front anti-roll bar. Oversize 6.95-14 U.S. Royal Loredo tires.

■ *The plastic and chrome steering wheel used in the Nova SS was anything but a high-performance type. The three-spoke design incorporated a chrome plated horn ring.*

1966 Chevrolet Nova SS Sport

1967
Chevrolet Chevelle SS 396

I n 1967 Detroit pulled out all stops to give automotive enthusiasts the specialty cars and equipment features they needed to fulfill their automotive passions. In the '50s, buyers had only one-size-fits-all cars to carry the family around in. By the mid-1960s, the market for various-size cars offering more than just basic transportation had tripled. There were small cars, mid-size cars and large cars and all types of variations on each thanks to a myriad of add-on options.

Alfred P. Sloane, Jr., had pointed out the importance of different color and trim choices and optional equipment in his book *My Years With General Motors*. According to Sloane, it was feasible that Chevrolet in 1959 could build an entire year's run of cars without making any two exactly alike. This concept became more and more important in the '60s, when manufacturers created muscle cars like the GTO by packaging certain options together. Big-block V-8s, four-speed transmissions, bucket seats, firm suspensions, fancy wheels, fat tires and performance axles could convert a family car into a street-racing machine.

■ *The simulated air scoop grilles on the Chevelle SS 396 ran parallel to each other longitudinally and were set into raised panels stamped into the hood's sheet metal.*

PICTURE PERFECT DETAIL:

Standard GM safety features. Flush and dry rocker panels. Inner fenders. Foot-operated parking brake. Carpeting. Color-keyed panel padding. Malibu steering wheel. Clock. Glove box light. All-vinyl bucket seat interior. Special wheel covers. SS identification features. Simulated hood air scoop. Special nylon Red Stripe F70-14 tires. 396-cid 325-hp V-8 (350- and 375-hp optional). Floor-mounted three-speed manual transmission (four-speed wide-ratio, four-speed close-ratio and Turbo Hydra-Matic optional). Heavy-duty clutch. Closed crankcase ventilation. Note: a console was available with three-speed manual transmission only on the SS 396 and the SS 396 was the only model available with Turbo Hydra-Matic.

■ *The SS 396 Chevelle interior featured a padded dash with controls and instruments laid out horizontally. A three-spoke steering wheel was used.*

Options "ruled" at GM and Chevrolet was particularly adept at putting nice packages together. Its street muscle car was the Super Sport, which was available for Sport Coupes and convertibles. It was originally a trim option, separate from any engine option. In some years, you could even add Super Sport content to a six-cylinder Chevy.

As the muscle car market grew, the package evolved and by the time that the SS 396 version of the Chevelle arrived, the entire package was planned around the 396-cid big-block V-8. You couldn't get a 1967 Chevelle Super Sport without a 396-cid engine and you couldn't get a 396 engine in a Chevelle that wasn't a Super Sport.

The Chevy 396-cid V-8 was the regular production version of the "porcupine" engine that Chevrolet had worked up for stock car racing. It was first released as a 375-hp motor for sporty '65 Malibus. For 1967 it was also merchandised in 325- and 350-hp versions.

The 375-hp version of the 396-cid V-8 was not listed on Chevrolet's internal specification sheets for Chevelles, but it was possible to purchase the necessary components from a Chevrolet dealer to convert the 350-hp V-8 to a 375-hp job. The cost of this conversion was $475.80. The 375-hp engine had an 11.0:1 compression ratio and a single four-barrel carburetor. The horsepower peak was achieved at 5600 rpm and the torque rating was 415 lb.-ft. at 3600 rpm.

A "dual-purpose" Turbo-Hydra-Matic 350 transmission was a newly available extra for the SS 396 only. This option allowed shifting gears with an automatic transmission, as well as "shift-less" operation in the "D" range.

The 1967 Chevelle body had only a couple of changes. The forward-thrusting front fenders had a more vertical feature line. The grille bars were thicker. The headlights were moved further apart. At the rear the "veed" taillights were notched into the fender ends. Ribs molded into the taillight lenses divided them into three stacked segments.

The Chevelle SS 396 had a youthful flair and was identifiable by its special black-accented grille with an SS 396 center badge, bright front and rear wheelhouse outline moldings, ribbed gray-accented body sill moldings, color-keyed body side accent stripes, a simulated hood air scoop with a new bright metal horizontal louver, Super Sport rear fender emblems on both sides, a black-painted rear cove panel (with an SS 396 center medallion), five special Red Stripe wide-tread tires and specific full wheel covers. The SS 396 interiors were all-vinyl, with a black-accented upper panel on the instrument board.

■ *SS 396 Chevelle hardtops were slightly more aerodynamic than the ragtop version. The 375-hp hardtop could do 0-to 60 mph in 6.5 seconds and the quarter mile in 14.9.*

1967 Chevrolet Chevelle SS 396

151

1969
Chevrolet Camaro Z/28
Sport Coupe

Whichever numbers you use,
the Camaro Z/28 was fast, especially
for a small-block car.

Car Life had a problem in 1969. The magazine wanted to do a test of all "Trans Am" versions of pony cars that carmakers were rushing to develop. The idea was that producing a certain number of copies would "legalize" the cars for the Sports Car Club of America's Trans-American racing series. To qualify for that formula, pony cars had to have under-5.0-litre engines.

■ *A Super Scoop added to the Z/28's hood took in cold air from the windshield's base. The scoop was made of sheet metal and the racing stripes ran over on both sides with body color in the middle.*

PICTURE PERFECT DETAIL:

[Revised May 1, 1969] Z/28 Special Performance Package for Camaro Sport Coupe. Dealer cost: $400.78. Retail price: $506.60. Includes 302-cid V-8. Dual exhausts. Deep-tone mufflers. Special front and rear suspension with stiffer springs and shock absorbers. Heavy-duty radiator and temperature-controlled fan. Quick-ratio steering. 15 x 7-inch Rally wheels. E70 x 15 white-lettered tires. 3.73:1 axle. Rally stripes on hood and deck. Functional front and rear spoilers. Four-speed transmission and power disc brakes required. Positraction rear axle recommended.

■ *Chevy boss Pete Estes said, "Boy, there are kids out there with money and when they hear how Mark Donahue cleans up in Trans Am racing with a Z/28, they've just got to have one for themselves."*

Chevy (302), Ford (302), AMC (290) and Pontiac (proposed 303) were working on their Z/28, Boss 302, Trans Am Javelin/AMX and Trans Am (without a hyphen) models. Chevy told *Car Life* it would supply a Z/28. Ford said it would supply a Boss 302 "when it was ready." AMC turned them down. Pontiac hadn't even started developing its 303 — and really never did, except for prototypes. So *Car Life* got only the Z/28

The Camaro Z/28 was cool, but not quite stock. It had a special intake with two 600-cfm four-barrel Holleys replacing the factory's single 850-cfm Holley. It also had rear wheel disc brakes. Sometimes you just can't win, but the editors had lots of fun losing.

Almost every Camaro book and Web site uses the performance figures that *Car Life* got in that road test, which recorded a 7.4-second 0-to-60 time and a 15.12-second quarter-mile at 94.8 mph, as well as a top speed of 133 mph. Strangely enough, as

■ *The stock '69 Camaro Z/28 engine was a 302-cid V-8 with 290 hp at 5800 rpm and 290 lb.-ft. of torque at 4200 rpm. It had mechanical lifters, an 850-cfm Holley four-barrel carb and dual exhausts.*

was pointed out in the same road test, *Car Life's* earlier test of a stock, single-carb '68 Camaro Z/28 produced a quicker 14.85 second quarter mile at 101.4 mph. "An E.T. of 15.12 sec. isn't slow," said the magazine. "But it's not the direction the performance fan planned on going when he bought those two carburetors."

Whichever numbers you use, the Camaro Z/28 was fast, especially for a small-block car. But its main attraction was that it was a racing car that was perfectly happy being street driven, as opposed to some higher-strung muscle machines that bog down and stall at every light. The Z/28 combined excellent handling with a powerful and responsive small-block V-8 and was a delight to drive anywhere. With its special deep-tone mufflers, it also made great noise.

■ *An under-the-bumper chin-type front spoiler was part of the Z/28 package and was one of the more effective spoilers tested by* **Car Life** *in its June 1969 issue.*

The '69 Camaro had new high-back bucket seats that were very comfortable. That was not the case with the tiny back seat. A two-spoke steering wheel was fitted. A padded dash had its various elements arranged in squares and rectangles, though the main gauges were circular dials set into squares. The gearshift for the four-speed protruded from a square in a mini console that also housed engine-monitoring gauges in trapezoid-shaped protrusions.

Not all 1969 Z/28s are exactly the same. On October 18, 1968, bright engine accents and Z/28 emblems for the grille, front fenders and rear panel were added.

Rally wheels were no longer specified, but wheel trim rings were. The price at this time was $458. On January 2, 1969, a tach or special instrumentation was made mandatory and the price rose to $474. On April 1 the specs were changed to read "dual exhausts" and wheel center caps were specified, along with a front valance panel and rear spoiler. The price increased to $507. The '69 had an extended model year and on September 18, 1969, the package was revised again, with the price going to $522. Bright exhaust tips were added. The final changes came November 3, 1969, and were minor. For the model year, 20,302 Camaro Z/28s were made.

■ *The Camaro interior featured a padded dash with controls and instruments laid out in squares and rectangles. The gearshift for the four-speed gearbox had a nice "old school" shift ball on top.*

1969
Chevrolet Nova SS 396 L78

Fast and inexpensive, Chevy
created muscle magic.

I n 1969 Chevrolet Motor Division dropped the Chevy II name, which had been
around since 1962. "Chevy II" had always sounded a little odd, as if the compact
car was a sequel, rather than a companion. Chevrolet then called its senior
compact the Nova. In reality, not much else about the car changed, other than some
trim items.

Like other automakers of this era, Chevy was really into the "building block"
system of changing the character of a car by adding extra-cost options. And why not?
Selling options was good business. They added to both corporate and dealer profits. In
many cases, the extras could double the price of a muscle car.

If you wanted your 1969 Nova to look just a little bit sportier than a taxicab, you
could start building a better mousetrap by adding the ZJ2 Custom Exterior option.
It included simulated front fender louvers with bright accents, body sill moldings,
rear fender moldings, black body sill and lower rear fender moldings, a ribbed rear
trim panel and accent striping. When added to a coupe, the package also included

■ *The SS 350 was an option package that included exterior trim items, some serious
performance goodies and the 350-cid V-8. If you wanted an SS 396, you added the Turbo Jet
engine to your Nova SS.*

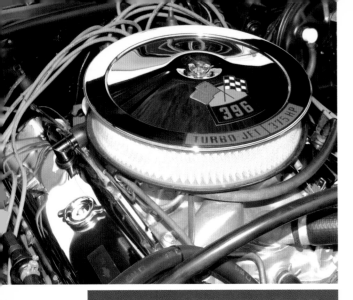

PICTURE PERFECT DETAIL:

[All Nova] Standard GM safety and emissions features. Front seat head restraints (mandatory option). Heater and defroster. Front armrests. A concealed fuel filler. [Z26 Nova SS] The base Nova SS (Super Sport) came with a 350-cid 300-hp V-8. Simulated air intakes on hood. Simulated front fender louvers with bright accents. Black accents. Black accented grille. Black accented rear panel. SS emblems. F70 x 14 red stripe Wide-Oval tires. 14 x 7 inch wheels. Special suspension. Power disc brakes. Special three-speed manual transmission. Bright engine accents. Hood insulation. [L78] 327-hp Turbo-Jet 396 V-8 for Nova SS ($316.90).

■ *Nova Super Sport models still had "SS" emblems decorating the front and rear of the body, but the "Super Sport" lettering that had previously appeared on the front fenders, where the new cowl louvers were, had to move elsewhere.*

bright side window moldings and lower body accents. Custom sedans got body side moldings with black vinyl inserts. The ZJ2 package cost $79 on sedans and $87.95 on coupes.

If you were interested in performance and wanted to add another building block, you could turn your Nova Custom into a mild muscle car — well actually a wild/mild one — by spending another $280.20 for the Z26 Nova SS package. This package gave you a fairly hefty 350-cid small-block V-8 with 300 hp, many sporty trim items and some important upgrades like fatter wheels and tires.

For those buyers who needed more go power, Chevy had a big building block — known to most enthusiasts as a "Big Block" — to add on top of the SS equipment. This was best known as the 396-cid Turbo-Jet engine. The 396 was a derivative of the "Mystery Motor" that Chevrolet had started developing a few years earlier for stock car racing.

Chevy not only offered this massive motor in the Nova, it offered both the "regular" 350-hp L34 version and the awesome 375-hp L78 version. This latter engine was really a pretty amazing option when you consider that just six years earlier, there was a corporate edict against putting engines with more than 300 cu. in. in a mid-size car! Now Chevy was stuffing motors with almost 400 cu. in. into

compact cars. It was quite a change and anyone interested in going fast for not too much money was very happy about it.

If you use simple addition (coupe + SS + 396) you come up with a price of about $2,684 for the higher-horsepower SS 396 package, but our guess is that most of these cars had another $1,000 worth of options (like a four-speed transmission, heavy-duty suspension, bucket front seats and so on). With tax, title and tags, you were probably looking at just shy of four grand for an L78 coupe, which was still the bargain of the century.

The milder 350-hp version of the Nova SS 396 coupe ran the quarter-mile in about 14.5 seconds at over 101 mph. With some super tuning, un-corked headers and racing slicks that same Nova SS 396 ran in the mid-to-low 13-second bracket. And the L78 had to be faster than that, if handled properly. Of course, not everyone in the world wanted to go quite that fast. Chevrolet could only sell 5,262 of the 375-hp cars, along with 1,947 of the 350-hp edition.

MUSCLE CAR • THE ART OF POWER

1970
Chevrolet Camaro Z/28
Sport Coupe

The answer to the foreign car invasion

The second-generation 1970 Camaro had an all-new Sport Coupe body. With a long, rounded, flowing front end, sloping rear window and truncated rear deck lid, it looked much more like a true European sports car than a pony car. There was a reason for this "Euro" appearance in that Chevrolet had the imported sports car in its cross hairs. Part of the way to make inroads against foreign cars was to steal their sleek looks. The other part of the equation was to go out and do some serious racing.

The Z/28 started out as a kind of racing car for the streets. In the late '60s, Chevrolet wanted to compete in the Sports Car Club of America's Trans-Am racing events, so it created the 302-powered Z/28 to "legalize" the model for SCCA competition. Back then, the SCCA formula capped engine displacement at 305 cubic inches, so the 302-cid V-8 slipped under the wire just fine.

■ *The styling of the Z/28 was often compared to that of a Maserati. One reason for this was that Chevy general manager John Z. DeLorean fancied Italian sports cars.*

163

Fat F60-15 Goodyear Polyglas GT Wide-Oval tires with raised white letters were installed by the factory on five-spoke Rally wheels. These new seven-inch diameter rims had a black center.

The 1970 (a.k.a. 1970-1/2) Z/28 package could be combined with the Rally Sport package, which included a different grille not covered by the bumper. The RSs used short, under-the-headlights bumpers.

As the '70s started, the SCCA revised its rules. This allowed Chevy to use the 350-cid small-block V-8 as the basis for a hotter-than-ever Z28. The 350-cid V-8 used in the "Z" was virtually identical to the LT1 Corvette engine. There was one difference — the Camaro had a more restrictive exhaust system. This kept output down to 360-hp. This was still better than one horsepower per cubic inch

The combination of the new body and new motor made the 1970 Camaro Z/28 an instant classic. The Z/28 goodies were actually included in a Special Performance package that retailed for $572.95. It was available for V-8-powered Camaros with special instrumentation, a four-speed manual or Turbo Hydra-Matic transmission, power brakes and a positraction rear axle.

In May 1970, Car Life magazine tested a Z/28 with Turbo Hydra-Matic transmission and a 4.10:1 rear axle. This car went 0-to-60 mph in 6.5 seconds. It did the quarter-mile in 14.51 seconds at 98.79 mph. Its all-out top speed was given as 119 mph. Car and Driver tested a similar car the same month and registered a 0-to-60 mph time of 5.8 seconds and a 14.2 second quarter-mile at 100.3 mph.

■ *The new 350-cid V-8 was dressed up with bright finned valve covers with internal oil galleries. These distributed lubricant more evenly to all of the rocker arms.*

Car Life got a little creative by organizing a "Showroom Trans-Am Championship" test that compared four American sports compacts against each other in acceleration, braking and cornering, using an SCCA-like point system. The Z/28 was the quickest on the drag strip. It did the quarter mile in 14.50 seconds with a 100.22-mph terminal speed. The Camaro came in second in braking and handling. On a road course, the Camaro was also second fastest. In all, it racked up total points and beat the Mustang by one point. "The winner is the Camaro Z/28 with 17 points," the magazine said. "One first, three seconds. The fastest car, and the more consistent."

The Z/28's 90-degree, overhead valve V-8 had a 4.00 x 3.48 in. bore and stroke. It was a true high-output motor running a Holley four-barrel carburetor on a special aluminum high-rise intake manifold. It had an 11.0:1 compression ratio. Other features included a pair of big-valve cylinder heads, a special high-lift cam, solid valve lifters and four-bolt mains. It produced 360 hp at 6000 rpm and 380 lbs.-ft. of torque at 4000 rpm. This motor was standard in Camaro Z/28, but not available in other Camaros.

PICTURE PERFECT DETAIL:

[Camaro] Side marker lights and reflectors. Heater and defroster. Windshield washers. Dual-speed windshield wipers. Inside day/night mirror. Left-hand outside rearview mirror. All-vinyl interior. Bucket front seats. Rear bucket cushions. Front disc brakes. Steel side door guardrails. Three-speed manual transmission with floor shift. Cigarette lighter. Carpeting. Astro ventilation. 250-cid six or 307-cid V-8. E78-14 bias-belted black sidewall tires. [Z28 Special Performance Package] 350-cid 360-hp high-performance V-8. Bright engine accents. Left-hand remote-control Sport style outside rearview mirror. Special instrumentation. Power brakes. 3.73:1 ratio Positraction rear axle. Heavy-duty radiator. Dual exhausts. Black-finished grille. Z28 emblems on front fender. Rear bumper guards. F41 Sport suspension. Heavy-duty front and rear springs. 15 x 7-inch wheels with bright lug nuts. Special wheel center caps. Trim rings. F60-15 bias-belted white-letter tires. Rear deck lid spoiler with Z28 decal. Special paint stripes on hood and rear deck.

1971
Chevrolet
Chevelle
SS 454
Sport Coupe (LS5)

It was, perhaps, the ultimate expression of a car made up of "building block" options.

I t was 1971 and the high-performance era was winding slowly toward its close. The "green" gang and the insurance companies wanted muscle cars off the street. And nothing else could have made the NHTSA happier. The latest Chevelle featured a redesigned grille with a chrome horizontal divider that separated the upper and lower sections and had a more "integrated" look. The upper and lower grille

■ *For frontal recognition, the Chevelle SS featured a black-painted grille, a special domed hood with hood locking pins and a remote-controlled Sport-style left-hand outside rearview mirror. Only single headlights were seen this year.*

■ *Mirror Magic acrylic lacquer was used to finish the bodies of the 1971 Chevelles. Chevrolet Motor Division claimed that this type of paint helped to keep the car's showroom shine." This '71 Super Sport features Classic Copper finish with black racing stripes*

sections still had four thin, bright horizontal moldings (as in 1970), but the number of vertical moldings was cut from 23 to nine. The reduced number of bars might have saved GM money, but they also gave the car a more muscular visage, since it was a hot rodder's habit to cut down on bright metal bits.

New single round headlights that were set in bright, square housings, replaced the twin and separated headlights of 1970 models. Here again, what might have been a cost accountant's idea played into the hands of the go-fast crowd, as two less lights reduced weight. There was a new front bumper design, too. The front parking and signal lights were twin-segment units, stacked on each other, that wrapped around the corners of the body. From the enthusiast's view, they eliminated those ugly add-on side marker lights.

■ For 1971, all Chevrolet engines (including high-performance "mills") had Controlled Combustion System and a new Combination Emission Control valve. Chevy claimed improved engine performance and exhaust manifold control.

1971 Chevrolet Chevelle SS 454

169

PICTURE PERFECT DETAIL:

[Malibu] All standard GM safety and pollution equipment. Astro-Ventilation. Cigarette lighter. Concealed windshield wipers. Bias-belted tires with tread wear indicators. Full coil-spring suspension. Perimeter frame. Advanced body mounting system. New finned rear brake drums. Flush-and-dry rocker panels. Double-panel door, hood and deck lid construction. Four inner fenders. Glove box light. Turbo-Thrift six or 200-hp Turbo-Fire 307-cid V-8. Three-speed fully synchronized manual transmission. [Z15 SS Package] Power front disc brakes. Black-painted grille. Special domed hood with locking pins. Remote-controlled Sport-style left-hand outside rearview mirror. Special heavy-duty Sport suspension. 15 x 7-in. wheels with bright lug nuts. Special wheel center caps. Wheel trim rings. F60-15 wide-oval white lettered tires. SS emblems. Black finished rear panel. SS instrument panel with function symbols. Cloth-and-vinyl interior (convertible all-vinyl). Matching door and sidewall vinyl panels. Color-keyed, deep-twist carpeting. [LS5] 454-cid 365-hp V-8 (requires SS equipment and heavy-duty battery at extra cost.)

■ *BF Goodrich Radial T/A tires were the popular choice of muscle car makers in the '60s.*

A new rear bumper with built-in taillights was used. Full-flow ventilation was standard on all two-door models. All Chevelles featured a new sealed side terminal Energizer battery. New interior colors and trims and a redesigned steering wheel were seen inside Chevelles.

To start building an SS 454, your Chevelle had to be a Malibu. This model name was normally found on the sides of the front fenders behind the wheel opening (although SS badges would replace it if you went that route). Included at no extra cost on Malibus were Hide-A-Way windshield wipers.

The '71 Super Sport package came in two versions called the Chevelle SS and the Chevelle SS 454. A glance at the engine call-outs under the SS logos on the fenders told you which one you were looking at. Base engine in the SS was a 245-hp version of the 350-cid small-block V-8 and a 270-hp "Corvette" version was optional. You could also get a 400-cid 300-hp Turbo-Jet big-block V-8 (which was promoted as an SS 396, but actually displaced 402 cubic inches).

The car we were "building" up to is the SS 454. It was, perhaps, the ultimate expression of a car made up of "building block" options. To get an SS 454, you had the start with a two-door Chevelle Malibu. The first step was to add the Super Sport equipment package. This was officially called the Z15 option and cost $357.05. On top of this, you next had to tack on the LS5 V-8 for $279.10 additional. Then, the T60 80-amp heavy-duty battery was required at an additional cost of $15.60.

If you wanted the ZL2 Cowl-Induction hood, that option was another $158. It included sport striping that ran up the hood, the air intake valve at the rear of the hood, the hood to air cleaner duct and the rear deck. Either white or black stripes could be had, except with a vinyl roof or if the roof was painted black or white.

■ *Vinyl-trimmed RPO A51 Strato Bucket front seats were optional in Malibu Sport Coupes and convertibles only and cost $136.95. A center console with floor-mounted shifter was $59. This car has automatic transmission and the N-type shifter is located in the console.*

1966
Buick
Riviera
GS Coupe
(425-cid 360-hp)

So the question arises, is the 1966 Buick
Riviera Grand Sport a muscle car?

Dennis Manners, the man who owns this 1966 Buick Riviera GS with the
425-cid dual-quad V-8, is a former Buick engineer who worked in the
carmaker's engine department from 1959 to 1996. "I was there when we
started the 425 and I did a lot of the engineering on it," Manners recalled. "I did the
option for the engine with the dual Carter carbs when I was only a kid in the business
— in the early 1960s — and the dual quad came out about 1964."

Manners drove a car like this dual-quad Riviera GS when they were new. Cars
like it are hard to find today. According to *Illustrated Buick Buyer's Guide*, the company

■ *The Riviera had hideaway lights that opened for an even more aggressive appearance.
Look at the aggressive stance of the Gran Sport. It has that "muscle car" look intended to
intimidate.*

■ *A low-restriction air cleaner with "Wildcat" decal is used. The progressive carb linkage allows the car to run on the two primaries of the rear carb. At about two-thirds throttle, the back two barrels and the front carb open up to deliver fuel. Note the finned valve covers.*

built just 198 of them. Manners first saw this particular car at the 1978 Buick Club Of America car show, in Flint, Michigan. The one-owner car appeared to be in wonderful condition. Dennis left a request to buy it under the windshield wiper. Several months later, he got a reply and was given the opportunity to buy the GS with 58,000 original-miles.

"I brought it home and spent 10 years just picking away at it," Manners said. The "picking away at it" included doing a little minor bodywork and a re-paint. The chrome trim and the interior are immaculate and untouched, as is the rest of the car.

The Riviera GS was no Buick luxury cruiser. When the first Riviera arrived in 1963 it immediately dented sales of the Thunderbird, which was the original "sports-personal" car. The 1963 and 1964 Riviera offered only a 425-cid 340-hp "last-of-the-nailheads" four-barrel V-8. The rear-drive Riviera weighed more than two tons, so the Gran Sport option was added in 1965 to enhance the car's "sporting" image. GS, in Buick lingo, meant "muscle car" and the package did not disappoint. The Riviera Gran Sport included a set of twin Carter AFB four-barrel carburetors that boosted horsepower to 360. *Car Life* magazine tested the Riviera GS and got a 8.2-second 0-to-60 and 16.7-second quarter mile at 87 mph.

Magazine test drivers must have really appreciated driving a classy car like the Riviera GS during the muscle era and they certainly appreciated its overall performance. *Motor Trend* took a '65 prototype to Willow Springs Raceway in early '65 and got

■ *Among American cars, only the Corvette had faster steering than the Riviera in '66. It required three turns lock-to-lock.*

■ *Even with column shift and a front split-bench seat the car's sportiness is not diminished. The dash is beautifully laid out and features a novel "drum" speedometer. Notice the custom style door panels.*

a 16.2-second quarter-mile at 87 mph, plus a 123 mph top speed. *Car and Driver* reported a 7.2-second 0-to-60 for the '65 and a standing-start quarter-mile of 15.5 seconds at 95 mph. *Road & Track* waited a bit and tested the '66 version. It did 0-to-60 in 8.1 seconds and needed 16.7 seconds to cover the quarter mile with an 86.7 mph terminal speed.

These figures were pretty spectacular 35 years ago for a big, heavy coupe running Goodyear Power Cushion 8.45-15s that would lay down rubber for several car lengths during hard acceleration. Manners said a GS would burn rubber for at least a car length and a half before catching hold, even on more modern radial tires. The best he has seen one of these cars run, with a little massaging, is in the 14s. He thinks 15-second runs are optimum with the stock engine and street tires.

So the question arises, is the 1966 Buick Riviera Grand Sport a muscle car? If you compare with other cars in its sales class, price range and weight bracket, it certainly stands out as one of the quickest sports-personal cars of its era.

PICTURE PERFECT DETAIL:

Heater and defroster. Directional signals. Padded upper instrument panel. Glove compartment light. Front and rear armrests. Front seat belts. Carpeting. Map light. Deluxe wheel covers. 325-hp V-8 engine. 8.45 x 15 black sidewall tires. Power steering. Power brakes. Safety Group. Accessory Group. Windshield washer and two-speed windshield wipers. Super Turbine automatic transmission. Deluxe steering wheel. Electric clock. License plate frame. Luggage compartment light. Trip mileage indicator. Rear glove compartment light. Safety buzzer. Glare-proof mirror. Super deluxe wheel covers. Back-up lights. Parking brake light. Tilt steering wheel. Lower instrument panel pad. Dual exhausts. Bucket front seats. Center console. [Optional] 425-cid V-8 with dual four-barrel carburetors ($188.13).

1972
Buick Skylark GS 455
Stage 1 Convertible

The good ones are all taken and the rest
of them have probably gone to the happy
hunting ground of muscle cars!

With its orangish red paint, white vinyl interior, white top boot, B.F. Goodrich Radial T/A white-lettered tires and Super Sport wheels, this rare Buick Skylark GS ragtop owned by David and Jan Hom of Missouri City, Texas, is one of just 81 such cars made in model-year 1972. The slow sales of this model had more to do with the waning of the muscle car era, than with any fault of the machine itself. In fact, it would be hard to find a cooler ride from that era. On a warm summer's evening David and Jan can lower the top, slip the Turbo Hydra-Matic 400 transmission into a forward gear and let the sweet-sounding Stage 1 V-8 pull the ragtop along as fast as they'd ever care to go.

■ *Dual, body-colored racing mirrors came with the Skylark GS. Bumper guards with rubber fronts were an accessory. Fender badges said "GS Stage 1." A "455" call-out wasn't used, since only the 455 offered Stage 1 tuning.*

PICTURE PERFECT DETAIL:

[GS] Dual exhaust system. Functional dual air scoop hood. Heavy-duty front and rear springs. Heavy-duty front and rear shock absorbers. Stabilizer bar. Wide bright rocker moldings. Front and rear wheelhouse moldings. GS monograms on front fenders GS monograms on rear deck. Black vinyl bench seats. Three-speed manual transmission. [GS 455] 455-cid 360-hp V-8. GS Stage 1 monograms in place of GS. Four-speed manual gearbox or Turbo Hydra-Matic 400 automatic transmission.

■ *Code WS identified the 455 Stage 1 V-8. It used an 8.5:1 compression ratio and a big Rochester 4MV four-barrel carburetor. It was rated for 270 SAE net horsepower at 4400 rpm and 390 net ft.-lb. of torque at 3000 rpm.*

Writer A. B. Shuman had a chance to drive a hardtop version of nearly the same car for *Motor Trend* for a drive report for the magazine's June 1972 issue. It was a red '72 Skylark Gran Sport with a white vinyl top and the powerful (and optional) Stage 1 V-8 engine. "Buick, it seems, has an indisputable knack for making singularly sneaky cars," wrote Shuman about his test vehicle. What he meant was that the Buick looked more like a warm-evening cruiser on the surface than a muscle car you would drive fast at the drag strip. The Buick looked every inch like the grand touring car, but the timing slips with impressive numbers that it picked up at the National Hot Rod Association's "Winternationals" drag fest in Pomona, California, indicated otherwise.

The Buick Skylark based muscle car had taken Stock Eliminator honors before it went on to whip all the other stock class winners to become overall category winner. Shuman must have raced as good as he wrote, since he made some very fast acceleration runs. His Buick did 0-to-60 mph in 5.8 seconds and the quarter mile in 14.10 seconds with a 97 mph terminal at the end of the drag strip. Admittedly, the car had some upgrades like open exhausts, fatter tires and a few other "tweaks" that NHRA rules allowed. Such "improvements" also helped weekend drag racer Dave Benisek set an elapsed time record of 13.38 seconds with the same machine at the famed Pomona strip.

By coincidence, during a test-drive a few years earlier the 1970 Buick GS 455 Stage 1 also covered the quarter-mile in 13.38 seconds. But the 1970 model had a

higher compression ratio (10.0:1), more horsepower (360 at 4600 rpm) and a taller (numerically lower) 3.64:1 rear axle. By 1972 all these things had changed. By then, the no-lead version of the car used a lower 8.5:1 compression ratio and produced 275 hp at 4400 rpm. It did come with a 4.30:1 rear axle, which made the acceleration runs that much more impressive.

"The amazing thing, considering all that's happened just in the area of emissions controls, is that a car that runs like the GS Stage 1 could still exist," Shuman pointed out. He called his mid-size Buick "the best example of the Supercar genre extant." (Shuman did have a way with words and was one auto writer who had more than just car stories published.)

Despite the good publicity in a big-circ publication like *Motor Trend*, Buick put together only 728 GS 455 Stage 1 hardtops, plus the 81 convertibles already mentioned. Just try to find one of those hardtops for sale today — never mind the convertibles. The good ones are all taken and the rest of them have probably gone to the happy hunting ground of muscle cars!

■ **Cars** selected the '72 Gran Sport as *"Top Muscle Car of the Year." Functional fresh air vents on hood provided ram-air action. The car had a heavy-duty battery to crank the 455 reliably.*

1972 Buick Skylark GS 455

1966
Oldsmobile F-85 Deluxe

Holiday Coupe W/4-4-2 (W-30)

High performance continued to be popular with buyers of Oldsmobile's F-85 and Cutlass models in 1966. The 4-4-2 super car option was in its third year and remained in high demand. Elements of the Olds muscle car package for 1966 included a specific grille, a distinctive taillight treatment, recessed front fender scoops and special ornamentation. To make things interesting, the 4-4-2 content could be added to five different types of mid-size Oldsmobiles.

Those wanting performance on a budget could turn the lowly F-85 Standard two-door sedan (enthusiasts call them "post coupes") into a 4-4-2. However, this was the least popular version. Only 647 were put together of which 490 had the base four-barrel V-8.

The Deluxe Holiday Coupe was a two-door hardtop in Oldsmobile's middle mid-size series. This car combined a customer-friendly price with the sportiness of a pillar-less hardtop. "Holiday" meant pillar-less hardtop in Olds lingo. Our featured car

■ *The 4-4-2 grille was different from the grille used on other F-85s. The grille insert had black-out style finish and a red-painted 4-4-2 badge was carried in the outer edge of the lower left-hand opening.*

■ *The 4-4-2 package included stiffer shocks and springs that made the high-performance model sit up high on its haunches. Red-stripe tires look great on a sporty red car like this Deluxe Holiday Coupe.*

■ *The Deluxe Holiday Coupe was a clean-looking, entry-level Olds hardtop that wore the 4-4-2 package well. Muscle cars were all about form and function, rather than chrome doo-dads and tinsel, so this rare version of the hot Olds was often overlooked.*

is one of the 1,217 units of this design made. It is also one of 178 with the optional Tri-Power V-8. The Deluxe came standard with rocker panel and wheelhouse moldings and upgraded interior trim.

The three other models available as a 4-4-2 were the Cutlass Sport Coupe (post coupe), the Cutlass Holiday Coupe (hardtop) and the Cutlass convertible. These came with a wider front-to-rear body side molding decorating the lower body feature line and were all more popular (or more common depending on your viewpoint) than the non-Cutlass version. With 3,787 produced (383 with Tri-Power) the coupe was still on the rare side. The ragtop had a run of only 2,853 units, including 240 with Tri-Power. So the winner was the Cutlass two-door hardtop, which went to 13,493 buyers of whom 1,171 got Tri-Power.

Getting back to the red car in this chapter, in addition to being one of the 178 cheaper hardtops with Tri-Power, it is also one of 798 that had an optional four-speed manual gearbox. Chances are that makes it around one of about 90 or 100 cars combining both options, but don't quote us on this, as it's only an educated guess. We can tell you for sure that all 4-4-2s with Tri-Power came with the four-speed.

The 400-cid Olds V-8 with Tri-Power was RPO L69 and it was a very strong motor. Magazine test drivers of the era always raved about these cars and talked about how they were the "Rodney Dangerfield" muscle cars. In other words, "they didn't get no respect." The package combined a 10.5:1 compression ratio with three two-barrel Rochester carburetors on an Olds B-head 400-cid block. For authentication, those heads will show a VIN derivative stamping starting with the symbol "V." The L69 generated 360 hp at 5000 rpm and 440 ft.-lb. of torque at 3600 rpm. There were two four-speed transmissions offered, wide- and close-ratio, both with Hurst floor shifters. With a four-speed the standard axle was a 3.55:1. To get a 4.11:1 or 4.33:1 required a dealer (or owner) install.

The Tri-Power option in an Oldsmobile hadn't been seen since the J-2 unit of 1957 and 1958, so it was neat to see the 4-4-2 offering it again in 1966. It's something that makes these cars special. Their performance was kind of special, too. *Car & Driver* magazine put an L69 with a standard axle to the test and came up with a very impressive 14.59-second quarter-mile with a terminal speed cresting the century mark at 100.55 mph. This beast also roared from 0-to-60 mph in 5.5 seconds. Of course, the magazine only squeezed out 11.5 mpg while tooling around in its 4-4-2. But, hey, gas was cheap back then and speed was king.

PICTURE PERFECT DETAIL:

Seat belts. Padded dashboard. Windshield-washer system. Two-speed wipers. Left-hand manual outside rearview mirror. Foam padded seat cushions. Carpeting. Unique 4-4-2 grille styling. Chrome front fender trim vents. Special taillight styling. Special 4-4-2 ornamentation. Optional high-compression L68 with three two-barrel Rochester carburetors (Tri-Power) V-8. 7.35 x 14 Redline tires. Optional Rally wheels. Four-speed manual transmission with Hurst shifter.

■ *A special taillight treatment with small differences from other F-85/Cutlass models was also part of the F-85 package.*

1967
Oldsmobile Toronado
Two-Door Hardtop

It's difficult to improve on perfection, which may explain why the Toronado saw relatively little change in its life.

The Oldsmobile Toronado was a "different" car when it arrived October 14, 1965. It was the first front-wheel-drive American car since the 1930s Cord. The styling combined a long nose with a truncated rear deck. The body looked as if it had been sculptured out of clay. A very strong feature line arched over the wheels and underscored the slab-sided looks of the body. The 15-inch wheels and tires looked huge.

The sporty Olds came in Standard and Deluxe trim. There wasn't much difference, but the brighter looking Deluxe sold best. There was no other car like the Toronado at the time. The sleek, ground-hugging body was poised on a large 119-inch wheelbase. Overall length was a big 211 inches. It measured 78.5 inches wide, but stood only 52.8 inches high. The 1966 Corvair

■ *The Oldsmobile Toronado was an extraordinary car in terms of its styling and character. It was the first front-wheel-drive American car to appear since the Cords and Ruxtons of the Great Depression era.*

185

■ *The 1967 Oldsmobile Toronado got a new egg-crate grille insert. The headlight "doors" were repositioned so that they stuck out more and lined up flush with the surrounding sheet metal body panels,*

■ *The 425-cid 385-hp Olds Rocket V-8 engine was standard equipment under the hood. It gave the sporty, but large front-wheel-drive Toronado hardtop an all-out top speed of 135 mph, which was quite impressive in 1966.*

■ *The addition of radial tires as standard equipment in 1967 helped to reduce the amount of wear on the Toronado's front tires, which was an owner complaint with the original 1966 model.*

and Mustang were the only lower cars around. Power in the first Toronado came from a reliable 425-cid V-8. The car weighed a hefty 4,496 pounds — about as much as a top-of-the-line Oldsmobile 98. It may have been sporty, but it was no sports car.

Considering its innovative technology, the Toronado got a warm reception from the press, especially in enthusiast magazines. It was written about a lot and the reviews were good. Model year production totaled close to 41,000 units, with buyers favoring the deluxe model 6 to 1. Toronado sales did not rival those of Ford's T-Bird, but they did impact the Buick Riviera's popularity. *Car Life* gave its "engineering excellence" award to Toronado. "Best luxury and personal car" was *Car and Driver's* **opinion**. *The Toronado was Motor Trend's* "Car of the Year."

Motor Trend took a Toronado on a 2,700-mile coast-to-coast test and averaged 13 mpg. The speedy Olds was easily capable of comfortable, safe cruising in excess of 100 mph. It took 9.5 seconds to scoot from zero to 60 mph and could do the quarter-mile sprint in 17 seconds at 82 mph. Its top speed was in the 135-mph range. In *Cars of the '60s* automotive writer Richard M. Langworth described it as "probably the most outstanding single model of the 1960s." *Ward's 1966 Automotive Yearbook* noted, "Certainly the highlight of the year in both engineering and styling combined."

It's difficult to improve on perfection, which may explain why the Toronado saw relatively little change in its life, but worthwhile improvements were made along the way. The 1967 edition was offered with two significant new options: front disc

brakes and radial tires. The latter were especially welcome, as the 1966 had developed a reputation for "eating" its front tires. Mechanical changes were limited to new-style driveshaft joints and, to soften the ride, revised rear shock absorber rates and spring bushings.

The long, heavy doors had been criticized; so door-opening assist springs were added. New comfort and convenience options included an AM/FM stereo radio with 8-track tape player and a center console (which negated the value of the hump-less front floor).

For faster engine warm-up and improved economy, a "climatic combustion control" system was adopted, along with Delco High-Energy ignition said to triple spark plug life, improve starting ease, and extend tune-up intervals. Appearance was spruced up with an egg-crate grille, headlamp doors moved out flush with the surrounding sheet metal, and revised tail lamps.

Prices rose by $100 or so to a base of $4,674. Though the Toronado remained as bold, brawny and beautiful as before, 1967 sales fell to about half the 1966 total, plummeting to about 21,800 (including just 1,770 of the standard models). Riviera also declined that season, though not nearly as much (to about 43,000) and the T-Bird gained appreciably, going up by about 9,000 units on the strength of its all-new 1967 design.

PICTURE PERFECT DETAIL:

All GM safety features, plus 365-hp V-8, Turbo Hydra-Matic transmission. Power steering. Power brakes. Cigarette lighter. Clock. Carpeting. Heater and defroster. Parking brake with parking brake on signal lamp. Deluxe steering wheel. 8.85 x 15 tires. Two-speed electric windshield wipers with washers. Back-up lights. Courtesy light package. Full-width Strato-bench front bench. Deluxe equipment included: Strato-bucket front seats with a pull-down center armrest. Chrome interior moldings for the windshield and windows. Wheel trim rings.

■ *Strato-bucket front seats and a center console were included as standard features of the Deluxe Toronado. This car also had added interior moldings and other small upgrades. Much-needed door-closing assist straps were added to the large, heavy doors in 1967.*

1969
Oldsmobile
4-4-2
Two-door Hardtop

Safety proponent Ralph Nader was having an impact on the auto industry in 1969, but Oldsmobile had enough guts to bring out several very hot, "slap-Nader-in-the-face" muscle machines like the legendary 4-4-2. Based on the F-85/Cutlass body, the 4-4-2 was Oldsmobile's answer to the Pontiac GTO and it was in its second year as a separate series. The 4-4-2 model lineup included a Sports Coupe (with a door post) for $3,140.85, a pillar-less two-door Hardtop or Holiday Coupe for $3,203.85 and a convertible coupe for $3,394.85. Where the corporate bean counters got the idea to tack on 85-cents to each sticker price is a fact lost to automotive history. Maybe it paid for their morning coffee. Total 4-4-2 output, by body style, included 2,475 coupes, 19,587 hardtops and 4,295 ragtops.

In one descriptive piece of promotional copy, Oldsmobile claimed that its muscle car was "Built like a 1-3/4-ton watch." Like the clock-gulping crocodile in "Peter Pan," the 4-4-2 ticked loud and precisely and was ready to snap its jaws at any horsepower

■ *Driving an Oldsmobile 4-4-2 simply gave you a touch more class in the late-'60s. This was the car that everyone read great things about in the car magazines (test drivers loved it), but only a few lucky souls could afford.*

■ *The 4-4-2 name was spelled out in large chrome letters across the body panel between the grilles. The '69 grille insert was made up of eight vertical oblong-shaped openings painted Argent Silver set within a rectangle on each side.*

■ *Heavier-looking styling was seen on the mid-size 1969 Oldsmobiles. When the 4-4-2 add-ons were done, the cars had an even heftier appearance with the dual air scoops on the hood.*

pirate trying to steal its go-fast glory. The 4-4-2 was hotter than just about anything other than the Hurst Olds model and it was a factory job with a lot lower price tag than that custom aftermarket conversion.

A new pitchman called "Dr. Oldsmobile" appeared in ads and prescribed image enhancements for the 4-4-2 in 1969. They included a bolder split grille, fat hood stripes and bright, new name badges. Also, the two-barrel "turnpike cruiser" option was eliminated to purify Oldsmobile's muscle car reputation. The base 4-4-2 engine was a 400-cid V-8 with a single four-barrel carburetor that pumped out 325 hp at 4600 rpm and 440 ft.-lbs. of torque at 3000 rpm with automatic attachment. If you went for the four-speed gearbox instead, like the owner of this car, the same basic engine carried ratings of 350 hp at 4800 rpm and 440 ft.-lbs at a higher 3200 rpm. Both versions used a Rochester carburetor.

A Hurst shifter was standard equipment with stick-shift cars like this one. Axle ratios were expanded, with some applications changed, too. The 4.33:1 rear, formerly standard with stick shift cars, was now standard only with the optional close-ratio four-speed manual transmission. A 3.42:1 axle was attached to wide-ratio four-speeds (as well as to cars with Turbo Hydra-Matic drive). The 3.08:1, 3.23:1 and 3.91:1 axles were back from the 1968 options list and a 4.66:1 axle option was new.

A divider between the halves of the grille, finished in body color, carried big 4-4-2 identifiers. The front parking lights were moved from between the dual headlamps into the front bumper below them. The bumper also had two open-air slots on each side of the front license plate indentation. Strato bucket seats, red-stripe wide-oval tires, a juicy heavy-duty battery, a dual exhaust system and beefy suspension components were included on all 4-4-2s. An anti-spin rear axle was mandatory at extra cost.

A 4-4-2 with the 350-cid four-barrel engine and four-speed transmission required 15.3 seconds to cover the quarter-mile drag strip and would be going 92.2 mph at the end. The same car could start from zero and reach 60 mph in 7 seconds flat. The 4-4-2 always seemed to be an "executive's muscle car." With its upper-rung Oldsmobile trimmings, the car just came in a cut above the low-priced three in overall level of sturdiness and quality. Unfortunately, it could never match the big-volume muscle cars in showroom sales.

PICTURE PERFECT DETAIL:

Standard GM safety features. Instrument panel ashtray. Rear ashtray. 70-amp. heavy-duty battery. Heavy-duty drive shaft. 400-cid 350-hp V-8. Four-speed manual transmission. Dual exhausts system. Carpeting. Wood-grain vinyl instrument panel. Instrument panel ashtray lamp. Chrome hood louver grilles. Special engine hood with two large, forward opening air scoops. Chrome wheel-opening moldings. GT hood paint stripes. Strato bucket seats. Front and rear foam-padded seat cushions. Bright front seat moldings. Heavy-duty front and rear shocks and springs. Deluxe steering wheel. F70 x 14 two-ply Wide-Oval Red Stripe tires. Floor shift with Hurst shifter. Heavy-duty wheels. Deluxe front and rear arm rests with bright accent moldings. Dome lamp.

■ *Strato-bucket seats were standard in the 4-4-2. Both four-speed and automatic cars came with floor shifters.*

More Defining Details of Historic Horsepower

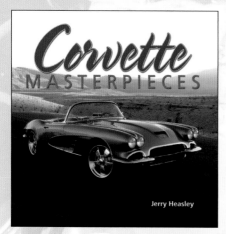
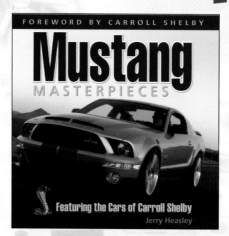
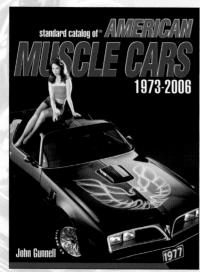

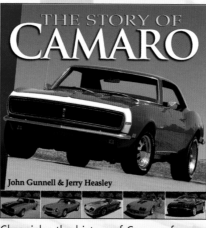
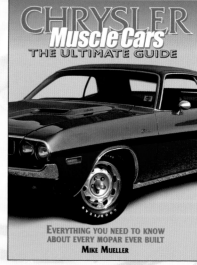